Life in Language Immersion Classrooms

Multilingual Matters

Please contact us for the latest book information:
Multilingual Matters Ltd,
Frankfurt Lodge, Clevedon Hall,
Victoria Road, Clevedon,
Avon BS21 7SJ, England

MULTILINGUAL MATTERS 86
Series Editor: Derrick Sharp

Life in Language Immersion Classrooms

Edited by
Elizabeth B. Bernhardt

MULTILINGUAL MATTERS LTD
Clevedon • Philadelphia • Adelaide

Library of Congress Cataloging in Publication Data

Life in Language Immersion Classrooms/Edited by Elizabeth B. Bernhardt
p. cm.
Includes bibliographical references and index
1. Languages, Modern—Study and teaching (Elementary)—United States.
I. Bernhardt, Elizabeth Buchter. II Series.
LB1580.U5L54   1992
372.6'5—dc20

British Library Cataloguing in Publication Data

A CIP catalogue record for this book is available from the British Library.

ISBN 1-85359-151-3 (hbk)
ISBN 1-85359-150-5 (pbk)

Multilingual Matters Ltd

UK: Frankfurt Lodge, Clevedon Hall, Victoria Road, Clevedon, Avon BS21 7SJ.
USA: 1900 Frost Road, Suite 101, Bristol, PA 19007, USA.
Australia: P.O. Box 6025, 83 Gilles Street, Adelaide, SA 5000, Australia.

Printed and bound in Great Britain by the Longdunn Press, Bristol.

Dedicated to:

Jeanine Baxter
Linda Blanchard
Blanca Cruz
Wanda Feliciano
Martine Legrand
Lisa Pinkerton Liss
Nathalie Maerschalck
Judy McCombs
Elvina Palma
Marisol Rodriguez
Patricia Roper
Pascale Scoyez
Alejandra Solano
Daniele Tuot
Philippe Van Minnenbruggen
Marilyn Videbeck

Contents

Introduction

Life in Language Immersion Classrooms is a book about teachers and teaching. Specifically, it is about teaching language by means of immersion; i.e. when language is taught not as a subject, but rather as the medium through which content material is instructed.

This theme of teachers and teaching may not appear at first glance to be anything revolutionary. But in reality, while immersion language teaching has been heralded as 'the most successful language teaching program ever recorded in the professional language teaching literature' (Krashen, 1985b:57), it has never been analyzed or researched as 'teaching'.

Immersion research has focused almost exclusively on the language dimension of language teaching or as Genesee (1987) puts it on 'product' or 'summative aspects' (p. 184). Genesee points out that 'it is rare...to find teachers trained specifically for immersion' (p. 18) and continues:

...there is a virtual absence of information concerning the pedagogical and linguistic strategies used by immersion teachers... Lacking such information, we are poorly prepared to train teachers in the most effective instructional strategies. A program of research to investigate how immersion teachers integrate academic and language instruction is called for...(p. 184–5).

This book documents such a program of research. It chronicles a two-year research project that involved the staff and principals of two immersion schools in the midwestern United States, in collaboration with a team of educational researchers, specialists in second language as well as in language arts teaching. The research on which the book is based was funded by the United States Department of Education, Secretary's Discretionary Fund for Critical Foreign Languages from 1988 to 1990.

This book is not about language analysis or about how learners in immersion programs can or cannot become fluent. These aspects of immersion have been documented through extensive inquiries into the quality of language learned as well as its relationship to academic and social skills in the native language. Such findings have been deftly summarized in *Bilingualism and Education* (Cummins & Swain, 1986), in *Learning through Two Languages* (Genessee, 1987), and most recently in *The Development of Second*

1

Language Proficiency (Harley *et al.*, 1990). Each of these syntheses indicates that immersion students acquire remarkable proficiency in the language in which they are taught and simultaneously perform in academic areas such as reading and writing at equal or superior levels to peers educated in monolingual settings.

But what of immersion teachers—the key players who bring about the immersion success? Who are they? What are their stories? How do they conceptualize the act of immersion teaching? How do they make decisions? What are their beliefs about immersion teaching? Why do they teach the way they do? How can a person become an immersion teacher? How do immersion schools function within the context of entire school systems? How are they maintained within the increasingly complex and confusing arena of public education? These are questions explored in this book.

The research program on immersion illustrated in this book was molded by two philosophies. First, the project was rooted in the belief that in order to begin to understand immersion teaching, significant and sustained probing of teachers' beliefs and experiences was critical. Educational research has a history of observing teachers, making lists of teacher behaviors gleaned from such observations, and then relating those lists of behaviors to student achievement. This model of educational research is called process–product (for example, Dunkin & Biddle, 1974). The undergirding philosophy of this research was, in contrast, that the only way to genuinely understand teacher behavior was to ask teachers about their behavior, to have them reflect on it, to analyze it, and to introspect about it.

Hence, the research reported in this book was conducted within a model of narrative inquiry; i.e. 'the study of the ways humans experience the world' (Connelly & Clandinin, 1990:2). We studied the ways immersion teachers experience immersion teaching in a variety of ways. We used field notes and videotapes and had teachers react to our records and observations; we also asked teachers to introspect or think-aloud while watching videotapes of themselves, allowing them the opportunity to react and respond to any feature of their teaching as they wished. In addition, we conducted structured and unstructured interviews about teaching in general and about immersion in particular. We also asked the participating immersion teachers to guide the research project. Through these different lenses we hoped to understand 'how practitioners make sense of what they are doing' (Carr & Kemmis, 1983).

Another hallmark of conducting narrative inquiry, though, is hearing the voice of the researcher. Rather than pretending to be dispassionate, objective 'observers', the principal researchers in this project were who they are—American foreign language teachers with conventional classroom language learning and teaching experiences (e.g. language as 'subject to be learned' on a four days a week, 47 minutes a day schedule) and with conventional training (e.g. 'how to present a dialogue' or 'how to conduct a communicative activity' or 'how to drill mechanically, meaningfully, and communicatively'). The perspectives, the beliefs, and the biases of these researchers were constantly at play through the project, and they emerge in the research findings and well as in the conclusions.

Parallel to this dimension of the research, is the belief among language educators that language instruction for children is the most effective and efficient means of acquiring proficiency in a second language. Methods used for child language instruction are frequently cited as providing models for adult language instruction in structured settings. As a result, these beliefs are at play in the discussion throughout this book, making the research in this book not only responsive to immersion settings, but also to a variety of other language learning settings.

The second philosophy undergirding our research program was rooted in the belief that immersion teaching was a particular kind of teaching— that it was not just language teaching. In fact, one of our consultants, Bernard Mohan of the University of British Columbia articulated the philosophy for us. He said that 'immersion is a whole curriculum embedded in a school situation. It needs to be viewed as such, not simply as a "way of learning French or Spanish", for example' (Personal Communication, 1989). For this specific reason we included in our research program questions about immersion as elementary school teaching and as language arts instruction regardless of the 'language'. In addition, we focused on administrative aspects of developing and maintaining language immersion schools within a public school district.

These philosophies are the impetus for the title of this volume, *Life in Language Immersion Classrooms*. 'Life' underlines our commitment to telling immersion teachers' stories. 'Language Immersion Classrooms' underlines our belief that in one sense all elementary schools are language immersion classrooms. Language is a fixed variable. The random element is in which language children are immersed.

Life in Immersion Language Schools consists of eight chapters organized around three themes. Part I consists of two in-depth studies of immersion teachers. Chapter 1, 'Immersion Teachers' Pedagogical Beliefs and Practices: Results of a Descriptive Analysis' by Ann Salomone reports on the initial study conducted under the auspices of the entire project. Salomone spent four months in an elementary French immersion school, observing and videotaping seven teachers, and then conducting stimulated interviews with each of the teachers. From these observations and interviews, she gathered themes which unify the behaviors of the immersion teachers she observed.

Chapter 2, 'How Many Wednesdays? A Portrait of Immersion Teaching through Reflection', by Carolyn Mendez chronicles the reflections of three Spanish immersion teachers over a six month period. While the Salomone study sought to identify commonalities in the ways immersion teachers think about and deliver instruction, Mendez' study focuses on immersion teachers as individuals and on how their individuality and their beliefs emerge in their understandings of immersion teaching.

Part II, entitled 'Studies of Immersion Classrooms', focuses on distinct dimensions of elementary school life. Deborah Wilburn authors Chapter 3, 'Learning through Drama in the Immersion Classroom'. This study is an outgrowth of one of the Salomone findings: that inherent in the behaviors of immersion teachers is an intense sense of drama that is necessitated by teaching content in a language which students do not speak natively. Wilburn reports on the use of drama, focusing primarily on one first grade Spanish immersion class, outlining the differences in language produced by students and teachers as they participate in a drama.

Janet Hickman, author of a number of children's books, contributes Chapter 4, 'Whole Language and Literature in a French Immersion Elementary School'. This report focuses on Hickman's study of a fifth grade French immersion teacher's use of non-graded, authentic French studies for use in classrooms. Included in Hickman's study are her views on using whole language approaches in the immersion setting. Chapter 5 is an additional contribution by Salomone. 'Student– Teacher Interactions in Selected French Immersion Classrooms' is a secondary analysis of her data that focuses specifically on the use of oral language by immersion students in interaction with their teachers while completing content-based tasks.

Part III, 'Preparing and Maintaining Staff for Language Immersion Schools', contains chapters written by teacher educators and administrators. Chapter 6 is contributed by Elizabeth Bernhardt and Leslie Schrier. 'The Development of Immersion Teachers' synthesizes a set of interviews conducted with both American and Canadian immersion teachers about teacher education as it relates specifically to immersion and indirectly to the education of all second language teachers. The study ends with recommendations for a prototype development model for second language teachers of young children. Diane Ging contributes Chapter 7, 'Meeting the Challenges of Immersion: The Role of the Foreign Language Supervisor'. This chapter chronicles the process of implementing immersion programs in an urban school system and of maintaining them against a backdrop of periodically conflicting forces. Chapter 8, 'Immersion: A Principal's Perspective' by Roger Coffman addresses the dilemmas of implementing a district curriculum in a non-English school.

Like any research, the research reported here should only be interpreted cautiously and within the framework of its particular setting. First, it is important to remember that the data were collected within an American school setting. The cultural context of the American school system as well as its goals and objectives clearly influenced the findings of this project. Any reader must recognize that immersion schools in the United States are in place for reasons of diversity and desegregation. They are not reflections of a multicultural, officially bilingual society as one would find in Canada. This also means that neither the teachers, the students, the administrators, nor the researchers on this project were motivated by concerns of national identity. Second, the participants in the project, the teachers, administrators, and researchers, were relatively inexperienced in immersion teaching. The schools in which the data were collected had existed as immersion schools only for three years. None of the teachers had more than five years of experience in teaching in immersion classrooms. The administrators and researchers had even less. This youthful inexperience was marked, however, by an incredible enthusiasm and curiosity for the endeavor of immersion schooling—building programs from empty shells and making second language learning work in a monocultural, monolingual context.

The seeds of this project were sewn in 1985 when I had the privilege of teaching a summer course in the Modern Language Centre at the Ontario Institute for Studies in Education. Half of the students in my course that summer were immersion educators who told fascinating stories about their lives as immersion teachers. Over the following years I came to know many other Canadian immersion teachers—David Jack, Roy Lyster, Andrea Alimi, Jacqueline Parai, Estelle Rannie, and others—who fed my curiosity and continually increased my esteem for immersion teachers. My colleagues on this project have also been touched by the immersion teachers they know and have worked with over the years. It is this personal interaction and experience that has driven the research questions in this project.

Many thanks to the individuals who helped us see this project to its completion. We are particularly grateful to Ronald Leithe and to the principals and administrators of the Toronto Public Schools and the Peele Board of Education for hosting several project participants and for allowing us to ask endless questions. We are also appreciative of the guidance given to us by our project consultants, Carmeta Abbott, Bernard Mohan, and Merrill Swain. They all helped us to see different aspects of our project.

Thank you also to Mary Armentrout who typed the manuscript and to Karen Angell and Mary Lavin Crerand who copy edited and proofed it.

But most importantly we owe our thanks to the teachers who willingly gave of their time to reveal their knowledge of life in immersion classrooms. Without their selfless commitment to the project, *Life in Language Immersion Classrooms* would not exist. We dedicate our work to them.

Part 1:
Studies of Immersion
Teachers

1 Immersion Teachers' Pedagogical Beliefs and Practices: Results of a Descriptive Analysis

ANN MASTERS SALOMONE

Background to the Study

Instruction in a language different from the native language of students is not a new idea. Mackey (1978) suggests that such a method for learning both academic content and the second language may date back to 3000 BC. The Romans and Greeks commonly used a non-home language as the sole or major medium of instruction. In England and France, Latin served as the language of scholars until the 16th century; in the United States, bilingual education dates to the mid-1800s and the establishment of German–English schools. It was not until 1965, however, when a group of Canadian parents began the St. Lambert, Quebec, French immersion school, that the concept of majority-language students learning through the minority language of an area was taken seriously.

In the United States, the Canadian experiment was first replicated in Culver City, California, in 1971 in Spanish. This 'early total immersion program' for native English speakers provides all curricular instruction in kindergarten and grade 1 in Spanish. English language arts are introduced in grade 2, and instruction through English is expanded progressively until class time conducted in Spanish and English is nearly equal by the end of elementary school (Genesee, 1987).

The early immersion program exemplifies the current trend of all second language instruction: *using* the second language rather than *knowing* about the language with bilingualism as the ultimate instructional goal. This goal has been achieved most successfully by early total immersion,

9

according to researchers both in Canada and in the United States (see Swain & Lapkin, 1982, for a comprehensive review of the research).

Early immersion capitalizes on the neuropsychological (Lenneberg, 1967; Penfield & Roberts, 1959), psycholinguistic (Chomsky, 1972; McNeill, 1970), and social psychological theories that find younger children better able to learn a second language—physiologically, psychologically, and attitudinally. The immersion approach succeeds because of the inherent *meaningfulness* of learning subject matter through the second language. As Widdowson suggests:

> a foreign language can be associated with those areas of use which are represented by the other subjects on the school curriculum and . . . this not only helps to ensure the link with reality and the pupils' own experience but also provides us with the most certain means we have of teaching the language as communication, as use, rather than usage (1978:16).

However, some researchers are concerned about the lack of accurate French speech in immersion students. Pellerin & Hammerly (1986) measured the French-language errors that grade 12 immersion students made and compared their results with those of Spilka (1976), who studied sixth graders from the original St. Lambert early immersion classes: 53.8% of the sentences that Pellerin & Hammerly's 12th-grade students produced contained errors, while Spilka's study of sixth graders revealed errors in 52.2% of the students' sentences. According to Hammerly (1987) these results substantiate the continued inaccuracy or 'fossilization' of immersion students' speech.

It seems obvious that research (e.g. Pellerin & Hammerly, 1986; Spilka, 1976; Swain & Lapkin, 1982) has most often emphasized the *product* of immersion programs: student achievement. Little attention has been given to the *process* of immersion education. In other words, teachers' behaviors have been largely ignored. In fact, few accounts of immersion methodology exist. The classic Lambert & Tucker study (1972), for example, devotes only six pages to descriptions of two-hour observations of each class in the St. Lambert school.

As immersion programs continue to grow in Canada and, more recently, in the United States, students continue to show excellent achievement in both content and language acquisition. An increased demand for immersion teachers accompanies this rapid growth and presents the need for more immersion teacher training programs, which, to be successful, depend upon well-informed teacher educators. According to Snow, 'The closer we get to capturing the strategies and techniques, the better prepared we will be to train immersion teachers' (1987:24). And, as Willetts asserted, 'both researchers and teachers need to know what actually is happening in the classroom. Therefore, more emphasis is needed on the process (observation and description) rather than on the product (results and assessment)' (1986:29). In response to Willetts, Snow, and others, this study describes specific techniques used by several French immersion teachers on a day-to-day basis and tries to explain why and how immersion instruction worked in this setting by examining these teachers' pedagogical theories and classroom behaviors. To address these particular research goals, a study of 'teacher thinking' was undertaken.

Teacher Thinking

Teacher thinking is a relatively new approach to the study of teaching. Its goal is to discover the pedagogical constructs that underlie the teaching practices of experienced educators in order to understand 'what is happening here and why', (Clark, 1978–79) and to form an 'image' of teaching (Clark & Yinger, 1987).

Several areas of teacher thinking have been studied by researchers: (a) planning, (b) interactive (classroom) decisions, and (c) implicit theories and conceptions. Previous research discovered that, in planning, teachers choose which 'routines' they will use. These routines are defined by Yinger as 'established procedures whose main function is to control and coordinate specific sequences of behavior' (1979). Routines are necessary for the teacher to cope with the complexity and unpredictability of the teaching environment. Further, Clark & Elmore (1979) found that during the first few weeks of school teachers choose the routines that will serve them all year.

Interactive decision-making research involves the study of dilemmas and uncertainty. Teachers tend to follow their routinized plans until teaching is interrupted, and they must either decide to continue the lesson or to change it. Generally, teachers choose to continue without changing their routines, according to Peterson & Clark (1978). Clark & Lampert (1986) also determined that interactive decisions are often made at two-minute intervals and that they may be made on an intuitive basis. These intuitive decisions show justifiable inconsistency at times: Elbaz (1981) concluded that teachers are sometimes inconsistent because they base their decisions on an appraisal of the context and their 'practical knowledge', which is comprised of the teacher's knowledge of subject matter, curriculum, instruction, self, and the milieu of schooling.

Teachers' implicit theories and preconceptions have also been studied by researchers: Duffy (1977) discovered that teachers have conceptions of reading that may vary in stability and strength and that depend upon the grade level being taught. Although these conceptions may change over time, teachers do act upon them. Janesick (1979) studied one teacher's classroom 'perspective' and found that the teacher acted upon her concern for creating, maintaining, and restoring a group. Morine-Dershimer (1978–79a) discovered that teachers' beliefs vary depending upon the time of year that they are studied. After observing and videotaping 8 teachers weekly for 12 weeks, Nespor (1984) concluded that teachers' reports of beliefs may be considered retrospective sense-making. Clark agrees, stating that 'journal keeping, clinical interviews, stimulated recall sessions, and articulation of beliefs and implicit principles of practice have instigated a new awareness among a few teachers. These techniques . . . may constitute professional development activities of the broadest kind' (1988).

In addition to professional development, teacher thinking studies serve to inform the pre-service teacher. By examining information about in-service teachers and their routines, decision-making, and pedagogical beliefs, pre-service teachers can better develop their own image of teaching.

The Study

The present search for an image of elementary French immersion teaching was, of necessity, a naturalistic or qualitative study. This type of research has the following characteristics: it generally occurs in a natural setting (usually in the schools); the researcher is acknowledged as an influence on the study; tacit (intuitive) knowledge is used as are qualitative methods (data are words); purposive sampling helps maximize variations; data analysis is inductive; grounded theory results from the data analysis; the research design is emergent (the design may be modified as data are gathered); outcomes are negotiated (analyses are discussed with respondents); research results are reported as a case study; interpretation is idiographic; applications of resultant theories are tentative; boundaries are focus-determined; and special criteria for trustworthiness (credibility measures) are required (Lincoln & Guba, 1985).

This study chose to focus on teachers' implicit theories as they related to their interactive decisions. Teachers at a one-year-old elementary French immersion school in a large midwestern city were observed and interviewed over a period of three months at the beginning of academic year 1988–89. Six teachers were studied—one kindergarten, two first-, one second-, one third-, and one fifth-grade teacher. Four teachers were Belgian, one was American, and one was French. Each first- through fifth-grade teacher was observed for two full teaching days and the kindergarten teacher for two half-days. Teachers were videotaped for two hours during their observation cycles, which were concluded with a structured interview. (See the Appendix for structured interview questions.) The two-hour videotapes were then edited to 30 minutes per teacher, and each teacher participated in a stimulated-recall interview—a viewing of the videotape by the researcher and the teacher accompanied by an interview based on questions prompted by the videotape.

Several methods of data collection were used in order to provide for triangulation, one of the credibility measures of qualitative research (See, for example, Mathison, 1988). Because both interviews relied on teacher self-report, classroom observations were also used to cross-reference information that teachers offered in the interview setting.

As a result of the data derived from these interviews and observations, several categories of behavior and thought emerged. Each category was analyzed for each teacher, then all the teachers' behaviors and thoughts were analyzed across categories. The resultant themes provided a general picture of the 'Glenwood' school community. (See Figure 1.1.)

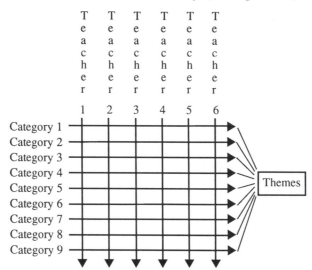

Figure 1.1 Analysis procedures

Categories

A list of 25 categories (consolidated into nine category groups) evolved as data collection continued, with modifications, additions, and deletions suggested by the teachers' behavior or comments. Because of the interrelatedness of many immersion teaching behaviors and theories, these categories sometimes overlapped.

(1) Teacher role—any activities that a teacher performs apart from classroom management and curricular instruction.

(2) Preparation—influences resulting from a teacher's training program.

(3) Experience—influences resulting from past teaching experiences (in either the first language or the second language).

(4) Personality traits—evidence or mentions of specific personality traits of immersion teachers.

These four categories were clustered into the category group of *Teacher Presage Variables and Teacher Role*.

(5) Content—references to what must be taught as specified by the school district's Graded Course of Study.

(6) Content comprehension input—techniques used to convey the meaning of content, including visuals, physical movements, English, simplified French, and frequent repetition.

(7) Routine—examples or mentions of the day's structure, boundary markers between activities, and specified subactivities.

(8) K to K (child-to-child instruction)—children's explanations of the teachers' utterances, given in either the L1 (English) or the L2 (French).

(9) Child-cued (instruction)—teachers' adaptations to the child's abilities, interests, learning styles, or needs, as well as instances of involving the child in learning activities.

(10) Comprehension checks—any methods that teachers used to verify comprehension in students. They can be visual, physical, or verbal—in the L1 or the L2.

(11) Units—references to or examples of the use of thematic units as organizational structures (e.g. Halloween, Christmas, the supermarket).

(12) Integration—lessons where more than one subject was taught in an interdisciplinary approach.

(13) Materials—mentions of materials production or evidence of it, including translating English materials, adapting French materials, and producing teacher-made materials.

These nine categories were combined to form the category group *Content Comprehension Techniques*.

(14) Reading techniques—specific techniques used for teaching reading (e.g. whole language methodologies, sight-word approaches).

(15) Writing techniques—specific techniques for letter formation and composition, including the writing process advocated by the local school district.

(16) Math techniques—specific math techniques, including the use of manipulatives, songs that involve mathematical concepts, physical

movements to illustrate concepts, and the use of math as a tool in other subject areas.

These three categories were grouped into *Specific Content Area Techniques.*

(17) L2 teaching—explicit out-of-context teaching of the L2, including sentences generated to teach a specific grammar point and references to phonics.

(18) L2 input—techniques used to help the children understand and acquire the L2, including simplified teacher talk; error correction; teachers' colorful L2 input; separation of L1 and L2; repetition; expectations of comprehension before speech, reading, and writing; games and songs; non-verbal clues; and encouragement of the children's L2 output.

These two categories were combined to form the category group *Second Language Input.*

(19) Organization—classroom arrangements that helped promote classroom control (e.g. desk arrangement and organization of materials).

(20) Discipline—any methods that promoted classroom control, including positive and negative reinforcement, clear directions, demands for student responsibility, teacher disciplinary actions, student movements (both to prevent misbehavior and to punish it), repetition of rules by the teacher or the students, efforts to please or displease the teacher, encouragement of mutual respect and self-control, use of English or visuals, student classroom tasks, and expectations of politeness.

These two categories combined to form the group *Classroom Management Techniques.*

(21) Outsiders—teachers' relationships with people outside the school community (e.g. parents, visitors, school district staff members, and university students).

(22) Team—the group mentality of the Glenwood staff, including the sharing of materials, ideas, and emotional support.

These two categories were consolidated into the category group *Teachers' Relationships.*

(23) Valuing of child—teacher behavior or references to behavior that improved the child's self-image (e.g. praise, tangible rewards, person-to-person conversations, accepting the child's emotions, physical displays of affection, and English to reassure the child).

This category formed the group entitled *Improving the Child's Self-image.*

(24) Culture—cultural transfer either by teaching method or by deliberate inputting of cultural concepts (e.g. mentioning French, Belgian, or

American francophone vocabulary) or integrating American culture into lessons. This category was called *Cultural Input*.

(25) Classroom surprises—incidents that surprised the teachers and would not have happened in a regular classroom where the students' first language was the medium of instruction.

In order to ascertain the validity of the categorization process, a near-native French-speaking graduate student in Foreign Language Education was asked to view two videotapes of one teacher during classroom activities and during her interviews. The graduate student and the researcher both tabulated behaviors and utterances that represented each category. Correlation coefficients of 0.80+ were achieved for each tape.

These 25 categories served as data entry units for PFS File, a data management system that operates on the Apple IIe computer. This system was chosen because of its capacity to accommodate lengthy quotations. All raw data were entered into the system, then sorted by participant and tabulated. Entries in each category were counted: Each ten data lines were counted as one occurrence or reference, and multiple concepts within one entry were counted separately.

These counted instances were tabulated for each participant, resulting in individual data matrices. 'ST Int' represents structured interview data, and 'SR Int' represents stimulated-recall interview results. Because both quantity and quality are important in naturalistic inquiry, frequent teacher behaviors and remarks as well as those that were particularly significant will be discussed.

Single-case analyses

Pierre

The kindergarten teacher, 'Pierre', was the only male member of the teaching staff. His role was that of gentle influencer, the staff member who initiated students into the behavior code for their six years of instruction at Glenwood School. Beginning-of-the-year comments reflected his belief in strict adherence to discipline tempered with genuine affection for the children.

While remembering that Pierre was observed only half as long as the other teachers, one can see that his observation data indicate the importance of a routine (25), adjusting teaching to the children's interests and abilities (child-cued instruction, 11), discipline (74), the teaching team (11), and activities that promote self-esteem (valuing child, 11). During interviews, his concerns were the importance of integrating content areas (8),

Table 1.1 Data matrix for Pierre

Categories	Total Observations	ST INT	SR INT	Total INT
Teacher presage variables and teacher role				
teacher role	5	1		1
preparation		2		2
experience		1		1
personality traits	11	1	1	2
Content comprehension techniques				
content	1	1		1
comprehension input	9	1	4	5
routine	25	2	3	5
K to K instruction	7		2	2
child-cued instruction	11	3	4	7
comprehension checks	4	1	3	4
units	1	1	3	4
integration	7	4	4	8
materials		2	6	8
Specific content area techniques				
reading techniques	4	4	5	9
writing techniques	2	2		2
math techniques			1	1
Second language input				
L2 teaching	1			
L2 input	17	5	4	9
Classroom management techniques				
organization of class	3	1	2	3
discipline	74	4	5	9
Teachers' relationships				
outsiders	7	3		3
team	11	4	4	8
Improving the child's self-image				
valuing child	11	2	3	5
Cultural input	4	2	3	5
Classroom surprises	2	1		1

the need for adequate materials (8), how best to input the language (9), discipline (9), and teamwork (8).

Addressing students in an unknown language in an unknown milieu required considerable patience, the only teacher personality trait that Pierre mentioned and one that was frequently observed. Pierre not only had an overall routine, but he also used frequent boundary markers between activities (e.g. songs and finger-plays) and was observed listing subactivities (with the help of visuals) for major classroom activities. Although Pierre recognized the developmental stage of his students, he chose to challenge them with higher-level analytical questioning (See Bloom, 1956) and by providing them with advanced tasks involving manual dexterity. Extensive use of visuals promoted these activities. Discipline, as previously mentioned, was his top priority, and one that was achieved largely through positive reinforcement. Encouraging students to explain activities to one another, using positive reinforcement, and believing in their abilities to perform advanced cognitive and physical tasks all supported Pierre's efforts to improve the children's self-esteem.

Pierre achieved the integration of language and different content areas by means of organizational units. A Halloween discussion included math (counting the calendar days and Halloween visuals), language (songs and descriptions of children's costumes) and science (Halloween weather). Tacitly acknowledging the 'silent period' of language learning, which has been documented by research (see Ervin-Tripp, 1974; Hakuta, 1974), and capitalizing on Piaget's theory of 'intériorisation' [internalization], Pierre often had students perform body movements silently while humming a familiar song in order to acquire language. He nearly automatically translated the children's English utterances into French, thereby also promoting their language acquisition. Pierre's participation in the teaching team was observed often, but during interviews, he expressed the desire for even more cooperation, team-teaching, and the 'whole school like a community'.

Denise

Denise's extensive teaching experience and reserved personality (the only French citizen in the study) may have influenced her interview data. She expressed few implicit theories, perhaps believing that such ideas were common knowledge. Because of their similarities in age and family commitment, she and the researcher had nearly automatic rapport. This, too, may have limited the ideas she felt compelled to express because she assumed that they were already shared information.

Denise faced a classroom of Glenwood School newcomers, many of whom had medical or emotional problems—a fact that probably increased the number of teacher role activities observed (18). Routine was a top

Table 1.2 Data matrix for Denise

Categories	Total Observations	ST INT	SR INT	Total INT
Teacher presage variables and teacher role				
teacher role	18	1		1
preparation	1	3		3
experience		3	2	5
personality traits	11	1	1	2
Content comprehension techniques				
content		1		1
comprehension input	5	4		4
routine	36	2	2	4
K to K instruction	8			
child-cued instruction	7	2	6	8
comprehension checks	6			
units	3		1	1
integration	6	5	2	7
materials	7	1	4	5
Specific content area techniques				
reading techniques	29	3	3	6
writing techniques	3		1	1
math techniques	7	2	2	4
Second language input				
L2 teaching				
L2 input	47	5	6	11
Classroom management techniques				
organization of class				
discipline	148	6	1	7
Teachers' relationships				
outsiders	10		2	2
team	13	4	2	6
Improving the child's self-image				
valuing child	9	1		
Cultural input	3	3	1	4
Classroom surprises		3		3

priority (36) as were reading techniques (29), L2 input (47), and discipline (148). Her interview concerns reflected her second-language-teaching background—L2 input showed the largest number of references (11).

Denise's flexibility ('I'm ready to change', she stated) was observed to be an asset in this relatively new kind of teaching with a new group of students. She was observed adapting activities (art instead of math) and methodologies (sight-word reading approach for phonics-based). Opening activities always included a discussion of the daily 'programme', and this daily repetition promoted learning, she stated. Because of the introduction of reading in first grade, reading techniques were observed often and included extensive use of visuals (e.g. child-made flashcards, teacher-prepared large animal cut-outs). Closely tied to reading, language-input activities involved songs, non-verbals, poems, games, linguistic expansion, and error correction by modeling. Discipline included both positive and negative reinforcement, use of visuals, withdrawal of privileges, student actions (repeating unsatisfactory behavior), teacher comments, and demands for politeness and self-control.

Marie

Marie's interview data, always in French, were extensive and consistent. Apparently enjoying the opportunity to promote immersion education, she seemed at ease in interview situations, where she verbally espoused immersion teaching theories, including ample second language input and implicit error correction. Her classroom management theories were based upon positive and consistent disciplinary tactics. Recognized as an exceptional teacher, Marie was recently given an Outstanding Teaching Award by the city school district.

Marie's personality was noted during observations (15 references); she also commented upon teacher role, likening it to 'une maman qui enseigne . . . à parler et à s'exprimer à un bébé' [a mother who teaches . . . a baby to speak and to express itself]—obviously a believer in the L1 = L2 hypothesis advanced by Dulay & Burt (1972), among others. Perhaps because her students had been acclimated to Glenwood the year before, she had fewer observations of routine (24) than Denise. Making learning fun ('Je m'amuse ici' [I have fun here]) increased her effectiveness.

Cuing activities to the children's level was often mentioned (14 times) during Marie's interviews and observed when Marie involved students physically (games of 'Jacques a dit' [Simon says] and intellectually (helping write the 'ours brun' [brown bear] books) and challenged them with more advanced activities when they were ready (replacing visuals with words). Integration of content and language was observed often (11 times) and discussed by Marie. She was adamant that this theory of immersion

Table 1.3 Data matrix for Marie

Categories	Total Observations	ST INT	SR INT	Total INT
Teacher presage variables and teacher role				
teacher role	10	3	1	4
preparation		4		4
experience		1		1
personality traits	15	2	5	7
Content comprehension techniques				
content	1	2		2
comprehension input	3	1	6	7
routine	24	3	4	7
K to K instruction	19	1	1	2
child-cued instruction	9	3	11	14
comprehension checks	5	3	5	8
units				
integration	11	2	1	3
materials		2	3	5
Special content area techniques				
reading techniques	16	5	3	8
writing techniques	4	2	1	3
math techniques	8	5		5
Second language input				
L2 teaching				
L2 input	35	2	15	17
Classroom management techniques				
organization of class		2		2
discipline	104	8	8	16
Teachers' relationships				
outsiders	14			
team	3	5	1	6
Improving the child's self-image				
valuing child	17	2	2	4
Cultural input	1	2	2	4
Classroom surprises	2	2		2

teaching be made clear through the study: 'De neuf heures à trois heures trente, je n'enseigne pas le français. J'enseigne des matières et le français s'apprend à travers ces matières'. [From nine until three thirty, I do not teach French. I teach subject matter and French is learned through this content.]

Believing that 'On apprend à parler en entendant' [We learn to speak by hearing], Marie was often observed (35 times) inputting French with carefully enunciated, grammatical language. She also mentioned 'L2 input' 17 times during interviews. Not only did she present the L2 through songs, games, 'comptines' [counting songs or poems], all subject matter learning, and classroom management activities, but she also required student repetition of many utterances.

It was in the area of discipline (with the goal of responsible behavior) that Marie was most impressive. Her students were required to reiterate classroom rules; and an individual student was often designated to monitor seatwork while Marie worked with a small reading group. According to her, 'Plus ils ont des responsabilités (s'ils savent les assumer), plus ils sont valorisés'. [The more responsibilities they have (if they are able to handle them), the better they feel about themselves.] Marie espoused positive reinforcement, which was noted over 40 times during observations, while only five examples of aversive motivation were observed. She also used vicarious reinforcement (see Dunkin & Biddle, 1974): when she mentioned the good behavior of one student, others also behaved better because they knew that it made her happy, she stated.

Because of her excellent classroom control, Marie often had visitors (14 instances of 'outsiders'). She was consistently kind to them, even those who interrupted her routine. Teamwork was vital to the Glenwood program, Marie thought: 'pour gagner du temps, et les idées . . . sont plus riches que les idées qui viennent d'une personne' [to save time, and the ideas . . . are more varied than the ideas that come from one person], and she noted that everyone at the school cooperated: 'On parle. On partage . . . avec le directeur, avec la secrétaire, avec tout le monde. On a tous besoin les uns des autres'. [We talk. We share . . . with the principal, with the secretary, with everybody. We all need each other.]

Supported by the large numbers of observational data in this category (17), one can infer that nearly every disciplinary and instructional technique Marie used led to the 'valorisation' [valuing] of the child.

Nadine

Nadine was the exception to the rule at Glenwood School. She was a spirited teacher who believed in teaching French *as a language* to her

Table 1.4 Data matrix for Nadine

Categories	Total Observations	ST INT	SR INT	Total INT
Teacher presage variables and teacher role				
teacher role	15	2		2
preparation		3		3
experience		1	1	2
personality traits	11	10	3	13
Content comprehension techniques				
content	2			
comprehension input	5	4	3	7
routine	17	2		2
K to K instruction	15			
child-cued instruction	5	7	6	13
comprehension checks	6	2	1	3
units			1	1
integration		1	5	6
materials	1	3	3	6
Specific content area techniques				
reading techniques	8	4	5	9
writing techniques	10	3		3
math techniques	10	2	6	8
Second language input				
L2 teaching	12	3		3
L2 input	77	1	8	9
Classroom management techniques				
organization of class	2			
discipline	77	5	4	9
Teachers' relationships				
outsiders	3			
team	4	1		1
Improving the child's self-image				
valuing child	14	2	5	7
Cultural input	6	3		3
Classroom surprises	1	2		2

second-grade students: Using phonics bulletin boards and sentences to illustrate grammatical points were examples of this tacit belief.

Nadine mentioned personality traits often during her interviews (13) and seemed to believe that a teacher's personality determined much of his/her success. Sensitive and intuitive, she cued her teaching to the children's interests (5 observations, 13 mentions), often basing lessons on items that students brought to class: 'Ça vient d'eux. C'est leur apport'. [It comes from them. It's their contribution.] Routine was important but not overtly stated (17 observances). Child-to-child instruction was common (15) and included child-to-child error correction, which was encouraged.

Most notable, however, were observations of actual L2 teaching (12): Verb conjugation posters decorated the classroom as did a poster stating, 'Nous faisons des phrases' [We make sentences] followed by sentences illustrating a verb construction. Indicative of her philosophy and orientation, Nadine showed obvious envy when the researcher stated that she was a French language teacher. Nadine also stated that she had each child read to her to 'make sure that they get the sounds right, they get the words right, they have the right pronunciation', again attending to language accuracy, which was observed in her frequent error corrections. She was also often observed using French in context (77), and both L2 teaching and L2 input were discussed during her interviews.

Nadine's teaching was artistic and creative. She illustrated story problems with drawings and had students imagine a 'grenouille' [frog] jumping from number to number in order to tell time.

Disciplinary tactics were observed often (77 times), but Nadine sometimes indulged her students, showing her articulated belief that discipline should be the parents' responsibility. Although she stated that she tried to 'reinforce the good attitude of a child', positive remarks were few, and observations of her doing tasks for the children rather than trying to teach them responsibility were many.

Genuine concern for students was visible in Nadine's classroom (14 instances of 'valuing the child') and mentioned often in interviews (7). She showed a deep affection for her students but did not seem to see her role as that of disciplinarian.

Patrice

Interviews with Patrice were forthright and productive. An uncomplicated person, Patrice seemed to enjoy sharing her experiences and beliefs with the researcher. Her theories about teaching seemed based on a desire to improve children's self-images, and she often marveled at their abilities. Also very physical in her teaching, Patrice clarified this observation during

Table 1.5 Data matrix for Patrice

Categories	*Total* *Observations*	*SN* *INT*	*SR* *INT*	*Total* *INT*
Teacher presage variables *and teacher role*				
teacher role	5	2		2
preparation		1		1
experience		1	1	2
personality traits	5		4	4
Content comprehension techniques				
content				
comprehension input	5	2	1	3
routine	16	2	1	3
K to K instruction	15	5	3	8
child-cued instruction	6	2	4	6
comprehension checks	14			
units			2	2
integration	1		5	5
materials	1	2	1	3
Specific content area techniques				
reading techniques	2	3	2	5
writing techniques	8	5	2	7
math techniques	10	1	2	3
Second language input				
L2 teaching				
L2 input	42	3	3	6
Classroom management techniques				
organization of class		1		1
discipline	52	3	5	8
Teachers' relationships				
outsiders	5		2	2
team	10	2		2
Improving the child's self-image				
valuing child	5		10	10
Cultural input	8	1	4	5
Classroom surprises		1		1

her interviews: she reported that she had previously taught physical education and in a class for the deaf.

Patrice's data indicate reliance on routine (16 observations), child-to-child instruction (15), and frequent comprehension checks (14). Although she did not list her daily routine, students seemed well aware of it, as evidenced by the query, 'Faire les mathématiques maintenant?' [To do math now?] Subactivities were also specified, as in the art lesson where Patrice listed graphically which parts of a landscape to draw in what order. She valued peer teaching, often matching experienced students with new ones. Comprehension checks were varied: visual (e.g. drawing a story), physical (e.g. standing to show agreement), and verbal (including literal recall, inferential-level comprehension questions, and evaluation) (see Barrett, 1972).

Because she was observed during a time when she was also teaching French-language sessions for an absent colleague, more math observations took place (10) than would have normally, but she was also observed routinely reading stories to her students. Writing activities (composition, following the system-wide approved writing process) accounted for the largest number of total references in 'Specific content area techniques' (15, observation and interview combined), and Patrice noted that the process is the same in English and French. Teaching underlying concepts was clearly the priority (see Mohan, 1986).

Patrice showed large numbers of observations in the categories of L2 input (42) and discipline (52), also. Obviously a proponent of the 'natural approach' (See Krashen, 1981, 1982), Patrice used gesture and temporal adverbs (e.g. 'hier' [yesterday] to show past tense and added that 'I'm just going to use it in sentences, and they just know'. She used modeling for error correction but refused to teach 'grammar' by telling students that they had made a 'mistake'.

Observations of discipline were less frequent for Patrice, probably because her classroom control was excellent, often involving preventive discipline (e.g. 'Qui m'écoute?' [Who is listening to me?] after which a show of hands was expected) and positive reinforcement (e.g. 'fantastique' coupons, stars on a chart for good behavior). A 'good discipline code' is all-important in immersion, according to Patrice, because 'They must look at you all the time and they have to be very patient'.

Instances of teamwork (10) and cultural input (8) were also relatively frequent for Patrice. She stated that she often conferred with American teachers about classroom management and referred to Belgian culture and that of French-speaking Louisiana.

With the largest number of mentions during interviews, improving the child's self-image (10) was a top priority for Patrice. She valued her students' likes, dislikes, and general mood and had students include this information in their daily journals. She offered weekly rewards and prizes for academic contests to reinforce their feelings of self-worth.

Estelle

Estelle served as a valuable respondent for several reasons: she is a native speaker of English (the only American in the study) and a recent M.A. degree recipient in Foreign and Second Language Education. She was therefore familiar with current foreign language teaching theories. Her metacognitive approach to interviews was especially valuable.

Estelle's personality traits were noted often (13 occurrences): patience, a sense of humor, clarity, reliability (the only teacher with a perfect attendance record), and intensity characterized her behavior. Her routine was clearly articulated (24 mentions): she discussed both daily and long-term assignments as part of her opening exercises; she clearly marked boundaries between activities ('Nous allons faire les mathématiques' [We are going to do math]; and she articulated subactivities carefully ('Il faut sortir la feuille de papier. Il faut numéroter de un à cinq. Il faut sauter une ligne. Il faut mettre "les mathématiques", la date' [Get out a piece of paper. Number from one to five. Skip one line. Put 'math', the date].

Observations of integrated lessons occurred often in Estelle's classroom (16 times). For example, a geography lesson about continents included a discussion of map scale and mathematical calculations of distances; and a lesson about time organized around the Olympics theme involved social studies, science, math, and French. Second language input techniques were noted 27 times and often involved teacher repetition as well as urging the students to speak French. Discipline (32 observations) was geared toward teaching students responsibility in preparation for their middle-school challenges: 'They have to realize that . . . the learning is going to be their responsibility'. Classroom management behaviors were generally consistent, except for one occasion when Estelle allowed students to go outside for recess after previously denying this permission—what would be called a justifiable inconsistency, according to Elbaz (1981).

Referring to several different francophone cultures and using vocabulary from each was conscious behavior for Estelle: 'I guess I've always thought that all of those are legitimate', she stated. Comparisons with American usages were also frequent.

Estelle mentioned child-cued instruction often during interviews (12 times), expressing the need to serve the children's developmental stage; and child-cued behavior was observed when students became involved

Table 1.6 Data matrix for Estelle

Categories	Total Observations	ST INT	SR INT	Total INT
Teacher presage variables and teacher role				
teacher role	5	1		1
preparation		2	1	3
experience		1	1	2
personality traits	13	1	5	6
Content comprehension techniques				
content		1	2	3
comprehension input	4	3	3	6
routine	24	2	2	4
K to K instruction	6			
child-cued instruction	8	1	11	12
comprehension checks	2	2		2
units				
integration	16	1	1	2
materials	2		4	4
Specific content area techniques				
reading techniques	2	2	1	3
writing techniques	1	4	2	6
math techniques	8	2	5	7
Second language input				
L2 teaching	1			
L2 input	27	5	10	15
Classroom management techniques				
organization of class				
discipline	32	4		4
Teachers' relationships				
outsiders	4			
team	2	4	2	6
Improving the child's self-image				
valuing child	2			
Cultural input	6	1	3	4
Classroom surprises	2			

with peer teaching, manipulatives, and experience-based activities. Estelle also expressed concern with L2 input (15 total interview mentions), stating that keeping interest up and facilitating learning while getting student participation was a difficult challenge.

Cross-case analysis

Table 1.7 shows data for all teachers. O represents observation data; I represents interview data. Teachers are listed in order of ascending grade level: Pierre, Denise, Marie, Nadine, Patrice, and Estelle.

Teacher Presage Variables and Teacher Role

Contrary to recent foreign language research, which found non-native speaker to non-native speaker interactions extremely beneficial to the learners (e.g. Pica & Doughty, 1985; Porter, 1986), Glenwood immersion teaching was usually limited to teacher-fronted activities for several reasons: the teacher's need for classroom control, lack of student second language ability, and the need for second language input from the 'only native speaker in the classroom' (Swain, 1982). Several Glenwood teachers expressed concern that more errors seemed to be committed in small group situations; for this reason, they chose to limit these activities. A large percentage of class time was spent in whole-class activities: 75–80% according to Pierre; 65% according to Nadine.

Parenting tasks occupy much of an elementary teacher's time; Glenwood immersion teachers were not exceptions. Physical tasks (sharpening pencils, cleaning desks, cleaning up messes); disciplinary tasks (setting limits and supervising behavior); and values education (instilling such concepts as politeness, morality, and responsibility) were added to the double intellectual challenge of teaching both content and second language in immersion classrooms. Although research conducted by foreign language specialists has measured the results of the intellectual challenges of immersion (e.g. Genesee, 1983; Genesee, Holobow, Lambert, Cleghorn & Walling, 1985; Swain, 1978), it has virtually ignored the multitude of other responsibilities that burden these teachers.

Glenwood teachers were prepared in various ways for the challenges of immersion: four of the six were trained as kindergarten teachers, while Patrice was certified as an elementary teacher, and Estelle's first certificate was in secondary French. Regardless of their training, all six teachers began at the same level of immersion knowledge, and most of them (four of the six) believed that prior observation of experienced immersion teachers would have been beneficial.

Table 1.7 Cross-case combination data matrix

Categories	P		D		M		N		P		E	
	O	I	O	I	O	I	O	I	O	I	O	I
Teacher presage variables and teacher role												
T-role	5	1	18	1	10	4	15	2	5	2	5	1
preparation		2	1	3		4		3		1		3
experience		1		5		1		2		2		2
personality traits	11	2	11	2	15	7	11	13	5	4	13	6
Content comprehension techniques												
content	1	1		1	1	2	2					3
comprehension input	9	5	5	4	3	7	5	7	5	3	4	6
routine	25	5	36	4	24	7	17	2	16	3	24	4
K to K instruction	7	2	8		19	2	15		15	8	6	
child-cued instruction	11	7	7	8	9	14	5	13	6	6	8	12
comprehension checks	4	4	6		5	8	6	3	14		2	2
units	1	4	3	1				1		2		
integration	7	8	6	7	11	3		6	1	5	16	2
materials		8	7	5		5	1	6	1	3	2	4
Specific content area techniques												
reading techniques	4	9	29	6	16	8	8	9	2	5	2	3
writing techniques	2	2	3	1	4	3	10	3	8	7	1	6
math techniques		1	7	4	8	5	10	8	10	3	8	7
Second language input												
L2 teaching	1						12	3			1	
L2 input	17	9	47	11	35	17	77	9	42	6	27	15
Classroom management techniques												
organization of class	3	3					2	2		1		
discipline	74	9	148	7	104	16	77	9	52	8	32	4
Teachers' relationships												
outsiders	7	3	10	2	14		3		5	2	4	
team	11	8	13	6	3	6	4	1	10	2	2	6
Improving the child's self-image												
valuing child	11	5	9	1	17	4	14	7	5	10	2	
Cultural input	4	5	3	4	1	4	6	3	8	5	6	4
Classroom surprises	2	1		3	2	2	1	2		1	2	

Although they had had little such time to observe, Glenwood teachers did have many years of teaching experience: Estelle and Denise had taught for about 20 years each, Marie for eight, Pierre for six, Nadine for five, and Patrice for four. This experience also differed in contexts, including kindergarten-through-eighth-grade Montessori school, elementary and secondary foreign language, Belgian kindergarten, and physical education and deaf substitute teaching. These differences in experience added variety to the teachers' classroom behavior and depth to their collective knowledge base.

This rich diversity was also reflected in the personalities at Glenwood School, but common traits of all six teachers were patience, diligence, commitment, French fluency, a sense of humor, sensitivity, respect for students, politeness, stamina, and adaptability.

Content Comprehension Techniques

These six Glenwood teachers all used facial expressions, body movements, concrete materials, and visuals both to impart knowledge and to verify its comprehension. French-language verbal methods of increasing content comprehension used by all the teachers included paraphrasing, relating new information to familiar material, reinforcing by constant repetition, using body-movement songs and games, and asking for child-to-child explanations. Student English explanations were often requested by the teachers, who, on occasion, used English themselves.

To structure their teaching, Glenwood teachers used integrated units. By focusing on thematic vocabulary and reinforcing it with activities in various content areas, teachers helped students learn to use the language in multiple contexts, a successful method for concept formation, according to Ausubel, Novak & Hanesian (1978). Although organizing by units demanded extra effort on the teachers' part, what was better for the children and the program was chosen over what would be easier for the teachers.

According to the data, the most often observed means for inputting content were routines, including the daily plan, boundary markers between activities, and sub-routines. Types of boundary markers varied but included overt announcements of activity changes, songs, games, and instructions to finish what students were doing. In addition to marking major activities, some teachers carefully listed subactivities, either orally or in writing, both to input language and to help students through tasks in sequential steps. According to Wong-Fillmore, teachers use '"lesson scripts" that they have adopted for each subject... For the language learners... Once they learn the sequence of subactivities for each subject, they can follow the lesson without having to figure out afresh what is happening each day' (1985:29).

Child-to-child instruction occurred in all classrooms (see Table 1.7, 'K to K'). Children not only helped one another understand content lessons, but they also helped the teacher socialize new students. Although they were quick to report rule infractions to the teacher and to offer their own disciplinary commands, they also encouraged one another. Following Mohan (1986), comprehension of content was further advanced by involving students as peer teachers: At Glenwood, teachers sometimes asked their students to judge whether other students' responses were correct, and they also placed individual students in front of the class in a teaching role.

According to Bruner, 'Any subject can be taught effectively in some intellectually honest form to any child at any stage of development' (1960:33). For this to occur, teachers must practice child-cued behavior— adjusting tasks to students and involving them in their own learning. This involvement was observed in all classrooms, supported by such comments as 'If they can act and be involved in the situation, they get a better understanding of it' (Nadine), and observations documented that Glenwood teachers constantly adjusted to the children's interests, past experiences, developmental levels, and abilities.

In addition to non-verbal comprehension checks (students responded physically or graphically), teachers used several types of techniques to elicit verbal responses: They offered incorrect answers to elicit correct ones; asked dichotomous questions (yes-or-no or a choice of two possible answers); asked for one-word sentence completions; asked lower-order questions about details; asked questions requiring inference; asked higher-order questions calling for evaluation or creativity; required oral or written re-tellings of a story; and gave paper-and-pencil tests. Either English or French was used for student responses because the language was not a priority; demonstrating comprehension was (see Swain, 1982:86).

Specific Content Area Techniques

Reading techniques. Although reading and writing techniques included the generic content comprehension techniques mentioned above, different methods specific to language arts at different levels were also used. All of the kindergarten-through-third-grade teachers read to their students regularly, ostensibly agreeing with Marie, who stated, 'Raconter des histoires c'est très, très, très important pour les enfants'. [Telling stories is very, very, very important for the children.] To teach the children themselves to read, Pierre conducted pre-reading activities with predictable sentences and pictograms; Marie and Denise used sight-reading techniques that emphasized word recognition ('la méthode globale' [the sight-word approach]);

Nadine stressed phonics; Patrice read classic stories to her students and had them base their compositions on them; and Estelle used group composition as a basis for a French-language reading activity. She also integrated French-language reading with math and science lessons.

Writing techniques. Exercises for writing can be divided into two types: learning to form letters, which is a kindergarten, first-grade, or second-grade activity; and writing compositions, which occurred at all levels. Compositions followed the pattern advocated by the local school system: pre-writing (discussing the topic and generating a word bank); drafting; revising (usually involving an individual conference with the teacher); editing (correcting French language errors and mechanics); and publishing. Stimuli for compositions included events in the children's lives, recent school activities, or stories that had been read in class. Re-telling of these stories in writing served not only as an exercise in composition but also as a reading comprehension check—a modified recall protocol (see Bernhardt, 1983).

Math techniques. Acquiring concepts, according to Ausubel *et al.*, requires that children of primary-school age relate 'their discovered criterial attributes to cognitive structure after they are first related to the many particular exemplars from which they are derived' (1978:87). Glenwood teachers were observed using various exemplars to promote the acquisition of mathematical concepts: fingers (to count on and draw shapes with); visuals (greater-than/less-than posterboard signs, various graphics); bodies (for counting); concrete materials (lunch money, crayons); and child-made materials (cards with geometric shapes). To serve more advanced students, teachers often used 'concrete-empirical props' (e.g. geoboards, place-value counting boards, and abacuses), which 'are necessary for concept assimilation' at the concrete-operational stage of development, according to Ausubel *et al.*

Second Language Input Techniques

Because language and content were generally intimately intertwined, most techniques used to enhance content comprehension were also used to input French. By far, the most important technique teachers used to input French in context was repetition, which was generally not simple repeatings of words but associated with visuals, body movements, or concrete materials. Nearly all the teachers used the word *reinforcement* for repetitions where the same words were used in multiple contexts. Not only was this repetition necessary for the children's concept formation or assimilation, but it was also vital to their language development.

The most common technique for inputting French was so automatic for the teachers that it almost went unremarked: translation of the students'

English into French. Besides translating student English utterances, Glenwood immersion teachers linked new knowledge in other ways to what the students already knew: teaching songs with familiar tunes, using and teaching second language words that approximated English ('professeur' rather than 'institutrice' [elementary school teacher]); reinforcing English lessons with similar French lessons; using familiar English games in French ('Jacques a dit' [Simon says]); relating new vocabulary to known vocabulary ('casquette' [cap] as a kind of 'chapeau' [hat]); and using new French words in familiar French songs ('Frère Jacques' became 'Où est Holly?').

Apart from these unknown-linked-to-familiar connections, the teachers' language input itself helped students develop linguistically. Far from simplified teacher talk, which may limit student progress (see Watkins, 1989), Glenwood teachers were observed speaking naturally, using relatively advanced grammatical structures (present subjunctive and future anterior verb forms); advanced vocabulary ('chatouiller' [to tickle]); playful language ('Gogo the escargot' [Gogo the snail]); rhyme; and figurative language, including analogy (singing slowly like a turtle) and images (making soup with scrambled words).

French grammar, vocabulary, and pronunciation were taught in context, 'as we need it', according to Pierre. If students showed ignorance of, for example, prepositions of place, a song taught them quickly (e.g. Marie's 'sur, sous, dans' [on, under, in] song). Other grammatical concepts were briefly explained: word order ('Rouge vient après' [Red comes after]); gender ('Un équilibriste ou une équilibriste, ça depend si c'est un homme ou une femme' [A (masculine article) tightrope walker or a (feminine article) tightrope walker, that depends on whether it is a man or a woman]); past tense ('Quelle est la différence? "Maman fait ou Maman a fait?"' [What is the difference? 'Mama does or Mama did?']); number ('Des, c'est beaucoup' [Some, that is a lot]); and pronoun use ('Que voyez- vous? Que vois-tu? On peut dire les deux' [What do you (formal or plural) see? What do you (singular or familiar) see? We can say both]).

Vocabulary was presented to further content activities. If a new geometric shape was included in a math lesson, for example, the teacher briefly mentioned its name, defined it, and continued the activity, because he or she knew that subsequent repetitions would cause student acquisition of both the word and the concept. Pronunciation was also taught in language the children could understand, with little or no theoretical explanation, as when explaining silent letters: 'C'est—le t dort' [It's—the t is sleeping].

Errors, which have been of central concern in previous immersion research (e.g. Lyster, 1987; Pellerin & Hammerly, 1986; Spilka, 1976), were of little consequence to these six immersion teachers. They were corrected simply by teachers' modeling of the correction, and Glenwood teachers seemed to know that students might or might not assimilate the correction, depending upon their stage of second language acquisition. Errors were not a problem for these educators, possibly because of the school's newness and the teachers' lack of immersion experience. If, after ten years of patiently correcting 'J'ai allé' to 'Je suis allé', they seldom heard the correct form from students, teachers would probably be more anxious about errors. At the time of this study, however, Glenwood teachers were not. Errors were corrected as grammar, vocabulary, and pronunciation were taught—in context and without theoretical explanation.

One problem in teacher speech appeared in observations of teachers in grades two through five: code-switching, a phenomenon that occurs frequently in bilinguals. According to Wong-Fillmore, a 'clear separation of languages—no alteration or mixing' is beneficial to student progress (1985:50). Nadine, Patrice, and Estelle, however, seemed to switch languages from sentence to sentence, and the reasons for switching were often not apparent. The researcher questioned whether this code-switching would put an additional cognitive load on students.

Encouraging student use of the second language (either by repeating teacher language or by creating their own) was frequently referred to or observed. According to Swain, output is essential to 'extend(s) the repertoire of the learner' (1985:252). To encourage student French output, teachers were observed using the following specific techniques: asking for repetition; reminding students to speak French; asking questions requiring more complex answers; offering incorrect answers to elicit correct ones; offering two choices of responses; waiting for responses rather than supplying them quickly; involving students as peer tutors and peer teachers; promoting written recall by assigning original dictionary activities; requiring memorization of a poem; and asking for descriptions of visuals. Although they did not explicitly state it, Glenwood teachers seemed to espouse Swain's theory of comprehensible output.

Classroom Management Techniques

Although references to the physical organization of the classroom appeared inconsequential in comparison to discussions and observations of disciplinary techniques, several teachers shared their ideas about classroom logistics. Pierre organized his materials carefully, and Marie placed the children's desks in a 'U' shape, a formation which was noted in other immersion classrooms (see Genesee *et al.*, 1985), and chose areas of the room that best suited their uses.

Of all the categories of behavior and thought explored in this study, 'discipline' was by far the one most noted during classroom observations (see Table 1.7). Whether such results would have occurred if the study had taken place later in the school year is an unanswered question (See Morine-Dershimer, 1978–79a, 1978–79b, for variations that occurred in teacher thinking depending on the time of year). Nevertheless, during the first three months of 1988–89, the single category of discipline was noted more often than any other during classroom observations. These notations progressively decreased from a projected 154 (77 half-day) for the kindergarten class to 32 for the fifth grade. It appeared that maturity and socialization to the school routine increased progressively from kindergarten to grade 5 at Glenwood, thereby reducing the need for teacher disciplinary actions or comments.

An examination of the use of positive and negative reinforcement revealed some interesting data: Pierre, Denise, and Patrice used approximately the same number of positive as negative disciplinary expressions while Marie was overwhelmingly positive, Estelle was somewhat more negative than positive, and Nadine was distinctly negative.

Examples of vicarious reinforcement (see Dunkin & Biddle, 1974) were common in Pierre's classroom: 'Regardez Robert. Il a fini. C'est bien, Robert'. [Look at Robert. He has finished. That's good, Robert.] During interviews, Pierre commented: 'You can easily say something like "That is nice. I like the things you do"'. Negative comments included threats of withdrawing privileges: 'Monsieur attend Mary. Mary, tu ne vas pas à la musique?' [Monsieur is waiting for Mary. Mary, you're not going to music?].

Denise also used vicarious positive reinforcement: 'Je vois Kathy bien assise' [I see Kathy sitting nicely], for example. During interviews, her discussion of negative reinforcement was centered around non-verbals— the warning poster, turning off lights, and names on the board. During observations, these non-verbals were noted often; however, some negative verbal comments, usually in reference to withdrawing privileges, were heard.

Marie's overwhelmingly positive data included praise and references to behaving as first-graders should: 'On se tient droit comme les enfants de première année'. [We stand up straight like first grade children.] Good behavior was often rewarded by privileges such as getting to line up first and listening to music. Marie was aware of her frequent use of vicarious reinforcement; during interviews, she remarked: 'Si je dis à un enfant, "Oh, mais que tu es bien assis", l'autre enfant se dira, "Oh, il est bien assis; elle est contente. Moi aussi, je vais bien m'asseoir"'. [If I say to a child, 'Oh, but you are sitting nicely', the other child will say to himself, 'Oh, he is sitting nicely; she is happy. Me too, I am going to sit nicely'.]

Nadine's negative comments were frequently noted during observations and were often combined with the use of English: 'Who dared speaking? I don't want to hear one more word until we get there' and 'If I have to say one name, you'll pass the long recess with me'. During interviews, she acknowledged this use of English 'for discipline . . . There is no way that I can make myself understood'. She did, however, try to use positive reinforcement: 'I try to reinforce the good attitude of a child'. Instances of this were recorded during observations, usually in the form of displays of physical affection rather than in verbal remarks.

Patrice's positive disciplinary tactics included tangible or visual rewards, but no vicarious reinforcement was noted, though American Indians were promoted as role models. Her bulletin board promoted students' self-images and their consequent good behavior by naming each student as the best at something. Instances of negative comments during interviews included Patrice's remark that she constantly reminded her class to calm down. Observed verbal negativity was most often in the form of threats of withdrawing privileges or subtle reprimands, such as, 'C'est pas tellement intelligent' [That is not very intelligent]. In actuality, most comments were neither negative nor positive, but more often preventive in nature— encouraging politeness, self-control, or consciousness-raising: 'Si vous écoutez bien . . . il n'y aura pas de problèmes' [If you listen well . . . there will be no problems].

Also an upper-elementary teacher, Estelle followed this preventive pattern. Comments and actions circumvented problems: 'We'll resume the French lesson when you are quiet' and a review of math facts while the class waited for a student to write on the board. Positive reinforcement was noted, however, and included applause for good behavior and frequent 'Bravos', while observed negative reinforcement involved staying in for recess.

Other disciplinary subcategories were noted in both observations and interviews. Instances of giving directions decreased progressively from kindergarten to fifth grade, with Pierre offering verbal directives nearly twice as often as Denise, probably a result of the intense effort needed to communicate with total immersion kindergartners in order to socialize them to school. Denise was more likely to use non-verbal methods. For example, she held misbehaving students until last for the line-up.

Student responsibility for their own learning or for classroom duties was a priority for nearly all the teachers, and these responsibilities were mentioned often. Responsible student behavior was observed as not occurring three times more often than it did occur for Nadine, however, because of her voluntary performance of tasks that students could have handled.

Teacher actions and student movement for punishment (both noted most often for Denise) were used in nearly all classrooms. All teachers used student movement games and songs to prevent misbehavior, however, with Pierre understandably using them most often.

The most interesting data arose from an analysis of how classroom regulations were communicated. Although students mentioned rules once in nearly all classrooms, in Marie's class they reiterated them on at least 15 different occasions. At her prompting, the students recited rules for hallway behavior and silent reading, when to raise their hands, why they had to be quiet during lunch count and attendance time, how to behave in the library and when Marie was reading a story, and why they had to be careful during recess. This student consciousness-raising seemed to have a definite positive effect on discipline, more so than when the teachers themselves reinforced rules of behavior, which Pierre did most often.

From interview data, we get a first-person account of the teachers' beliefs about discipline. Estelle spoke about students' responsibility for learning and for classroom tasks; Patrice emphasized student self-control and the importance of paying attention; Nadine spoke at length about responsibility and positive reinforcement, but her observational data did not reflect these concerns; Marie discussed responsibility, respect for others, politeness, and being consistent and positive; Denise mentioned the extent of Glenwood's discipline, student jobs, and non-verbal communications of her displeasure; and Pierre spoke at length about positive reinforcement but admitted that it was 'limited to physical expression' and simple French phrases at his students' level.

During the stimulated recall interviews, Marie seemed pleased to notice her own positive behavior. Nadine, however, appeared to have her consciousness raised differently as she noticed how many times someone said 'sh', to which she remarked, 'C'est fou'. [That's crazy.] According to Clark (1988), this type of consciousness-raising is a valuable result of studies such as this one, with the possible outcome of improved classroom behavior.

Teachers' Relationships

Visitors to Glenwood School were commonplace and welcome. Every room had a chair with a 'visiteur' label, and the chair was often occupied. Parents, other teachers, staff from the local school system, francophone visitors from other countries, women's groups, high school French classes, university students, and curiosity seekers were frequently seen at Glenwood.

Parental support was considered an integral part of the program. Nearly all teachers communicated with parents by sending student folders home weekly for signatures, and teachers with concerns often telephoned parents. In addition, over 50 parents volunteered at Glenwood in 1987–88.

Glenwood teachers were a close-knit group, as evidenced by their refusal to call a colleague's long-term substitute teacher anything but 'l'autre dame' [the other woman]. Mr. Loffland, the principal, promoted this closed fraternity by requiring all visitors, even those giving workshops, to wear an identifying visitor's button. The fraternity included staff as well: the secretary participated by making announcements in the principal's absence; the aide helped with materials and playground supervision; and the head custodian disciplined children frequently.

All teachers commented upon their team spirit during interviews, and their camaraderie went beyond the classroom: celebrating personal milestones, giving mutual support, joking, and socializing after school all encouraged team spirit. This *esprit de corps* was so pervasive that the teachers chose the following proverb for the welcoming sign at Open House: 'A plusieurs mains, l'ouvrage avance'. [Many hands make light work.]

Improving the Child's Self-Image

Placing children in an environment where they cannot communicate on their usual linguistic level can be a brutal blow to their self-images. Well aware of the difficulty of the situation, Glenwood teachers tried hard to give emotional support to the children. They lessened the children's frustration by allowing them to speak their native language; and by sometimes speaking to them in English, the teachers showed that they appreciated the children's accomplishments at their particular ability level.

Sharing feelings, concerns, and discussions of personal matters all showed the human-to-human relationships of Glenwood teachers and their students. The goal was to make the students feel good about themselves by valuing them—their language, their feelings, their classroom contributions, their good behavior, their lifestyles, and themselves—as young human beings.

Cultural Input

Although the European Glenwood teachers had been influenced by many American teaching methods (e.g. the writing process, whole-language philosophies, discovery learning), they tended to continue some European techniques, such as self-controlled physical education activities and Belgian math concept teaching.

According to Saville-Troike, second language acquisition must be seen as 'part of a larger whole—the acquisition of a second culture' (1985:58). This acquisition was one of the goals of the school: the European teachers often discussed their native culture. All the Glenwood teachers also tried to present Belgian, French, Canadian, and American francophone expressions of the same concepts. Because weather expressions, number names, and general vocabulary varied, all were taught, and the students seemed to choose which ones they preferred.

Classroom Surprises

Misunderstandings can occur in any elementary classroom, but those that happened in this immersion school related to the students' lack of second language knowledge (misunderstandings of words or directions), their metalinguistic abilities (questioning grammatical points), their positive attitudes (wanting to speak French), their acquisition of un-taught phrases, or their offering of misunderstood second language examples.

Conclusion

According to Stern, 'The question we should now ask is no longer: "How much better is immersion French than the French of students conventionally taught?"' His opinion, and that of most immersion researchers, is that 'the immersed student knows more French than students in other types of programs'. Instead, Stern adds, we should ask what levels of French can be expected at different times in the immersion program, for how long the French is maintained, what levels of French are adequate for comprehending different school subjects, and 'Is the level of French . . . the best that can be attained in this type of program, or could it be further improved?' (1978:846–7). Level of second language attainment has been the utmost concern of previous immersion researchers.

Data from this study, however, suggest that the level of second language attainment is a secondary concern for these teachers compared to achievement in other areas. Based on both the quantity and the intensity of their verbal reports and the observational data, one would judge that these immersion teachers believe discipline to be their top priority (at least at the time of year when the study was conducted), with content learning second, and second language attainment third.

The cross-category themes that emerged from observation and interview data reflect these priorities:

(1) *Glenwood teachers were a unique team.* Isolated in their cultural island and limited by the dearth of francophone support personnel, Glenwood teachers accepted their central roles in largely teacher-fronted classrooms. They blended several cultures, types of preparation, teaching experiences, and personalities, all of which enriched their classroom performance. Supported by parents and the Glenwood staff, these six

immersion teachers shared the immersion philosophy, linguistic expertise, classroom management techniques, attitudes toward discipline, teaching methodologies, materials, and emotional support.

(2) *Glenwood teachers presented content through the second language.* Common techniques were used for facilitating the comprehension and acquisition of both the local school system's required content and the second language, with concept development valued above second language progress. Thematic units, daily routines, boundary markers between activities, and specified subactivities structured the day's lessons. Linking the unknown to the known and using repetition, concrete referents, non-verbals, integrated subject-matter lessons, and student involvement all served to input both language and content. Frequent comprehension checks were visual, physical, spoken or written in either language, and at all levels of questioning in short or long responses.

(3) *Glenwood immersion teaching challenged the creative and adaptive abilities of its teachers as they addressed the varying and changing needs of their students.* Glenwood teachers adapted French materials; translated English materials; attended to the details of elementary school life; demonstrated content; provided concrete materials; focused on the learners' needs, interests, and abilities; allowed for frequent observations and student teachers; adapted to the American culture and school context; and changed methods or activities as the children required. This demanded extraordinary sensitivity and perception from the teacher as well as a willingness to modify plans, intervene with remediation when necessary, and offer challenges to promote student progress.

(4) *Glenwood teachers involved the students in learning and teaching content, language, and discipline.* Glenwood students profited from involvement in their own learning with hands-on, discovery-based math and science; experienced-based, whole language reading and writing; and both verbal and non-verbal second language activities. They also participated in teaching other students by explaining to one another, directing learning activities, providing corrections, and socializing other students to the Glenwood schooling process. Classes where students reiterated classroom regulations seemed most successful in this effort.

(5) *Glenwood teachers spent a large percentage of their time in classroom management activities.* While acknowledging that data collection occurred during the fall, one must still recognize the overwhelming preponderance of disciplinary data. Teachers generally tried to follow the principal's belief in positive reinforcement and consistency; some were more successful than others, but all seemed to accept this philosophy by providing positive role models. Aversive motivation was often in vis-

ual or physical form, and preventive measures were valued over corrective ones.

(6) *Glenwood teachers presented the second language in an acquisition environment.* While integrating several francophone cultures, Glenwood teachers promoted the acquisition of the second language with translation, rich language, non-verbal clues, repetition, authentic children's literature, songs, and games. Grammar, vocabulary, and pronunciation were usually offered only in context, and errors were corrected by teacher modeling. Students were encouraged to use the second language but not forced to do so. Teachers tried to keep English and French utterances separate, though their balanced-bilingual habits sometimes interfered. Classroom surprises generally resulted from second language misunderstandings, metalinguistic awareness, or positive student attitudes; and they helped Glenwood teachers retain their sense of humor.

(7) *Glenwood's immersion program was much more than a program for teaching language and content; it was a commitment to the development of the whole child.* Glenwood teachers performed parenting tasks; disciplined to teach responsibility, self-control, and mutual respect; offered content that prepared the child for life; presented the second language in ways that enriched and expanded the child's world; and strove to improve each child's self-image. All the teachers contributed their unique emphases to the program, and all the Glenwood teachers knew that they were shaping the futures of their students.

Limitations

Primarily descriptive in nature, this study explored the presage and process variables of six elementary French immersion teachers (see Dunkin & Biddle, 1974:38) and their related thoughts. The analysis of categorized observational and interview data revealed the teachers' espoused theories. When these verbalized or inferred theories were compared with the theories that they used, few inconsistencies were revealed: Glenwood teachers, generally speaking, were aware of what they were doing and could articulate why they did it.

As a contribution to the Teacher Thinking Literature, this study supports the conclusion that teachers do have conceptions of their subject matter (see Duffy, 1977). Similar to a later related study (see Bawden, Burke & Duffy, 1979), the present exploration also discovered that some teachers possess more complex conceptions of their subjects and that these conceptions may vary in stability.

As a contribution to immersion research, this study fills a reported void in the literature. To complement prior and on-going research on French immersion students' achievements, this study reports on the processes of immersion teaching and the theories that underlie these behaviors.

One must remember, however, that this is a study of process at one particular elementary immersion school. As such, its limitations are clear. Generalizing the themes or categories of behavior and thought that emerged from this study would be dangerous, indeed. As a qualitative exploration of the behaviors and thoughts of these six Glenwood teachers, this study must serve only as description, not as prescription.

Appendix 1.1 Structured Interview Questions

(These interviews were conducted in French or in English, following the preference of the teacher being interviewed.)

(1) What preparation have you had for immersion teaching?
(2) Do you think that this preparation was appropriate?
(3) What other preparation might have helped you?
(4) Where did you teach before coming to Glenwood? For how long?
(5) Was last year at Glenwood your first year of immersion teaching?
(6) How is this year different from last year?
(7) Please describe a typical day in your classroom (or yesterday).
(8) As a 5th (4th, 3rd, 2nd) grade teacher, how much of your day is spent in French?
(9) What methods do you use to ensure comprehension when you are speaking French?
(10) What do you do if a student seems not to understand?
(11) Describe some techniques that you use for reading activities.
(12) Why do you use these techniques? Where did you learn them?
(13) Describe some techniques that you use for math.
(14) Why do you use them? Where did you learn them?
(15) Describe some techniques that you use for writing.
(16) Why do you use them? Where did you learn them?
(17) If a student makes an error in French, how do you correct it?
(18) Give some examples of how you integrate content and language teaching.
(19) How does the immersion philosophy change the teaching/learning process?
(20) Do you ever use English outside of English lessons? When and why?
(21) What are some of the ways you organize your classroom?
(22) What methods do you use to control student behavior? Did you use the same methods in your prior teaching?

(23) About how many hours per week do you spend in materials preparation?

(24) What kinds of materials do you have to prepare?

(25) When do you work with NS (native-speaker) or NNS (non-native-speaker) teachers?

(26) What do you think are the advantages of being a NS (NNS) teacher in an immersion setting?

(27) What are the disadvantages?

(28) How is your immersion school teaching different from your prior teaching?

(29) How is this school different from other schools where you have taught?

(30) Can you give an example of something that happened in your class that was a 'surprise' that wouldn't have happened in a regular classroom?

2 How Many Wednesdays? A Portrait of Immersion Teaching through Reflection

CAROLYN MENDEZ

'Hoy es'.... [Today is...]

'¡Miércoles!' [Wednesday!]

The day is bright and, for January, unseasonably warm: 47 degrees. Barbara Cano invites her second-grade class to peer outside, beneath the broad manila window shade, and comment on the weather. The students are accustomed to this morning ritual and respond in varying ways, some more willing than others. Then the window shade falls again, and Barbara stretches the conversation.

'¿Cuántos miércoles hay en este mes [How many Wednesdays are in this month]?' she queries.

A high voice shrieks out, excited, after a general silence: '¡Cuatro!'

'¡Cinco!' cries another.

'Cinco', affirms Barbara, and together the class explores the wall calendar, just to be sure.

Morning has begun at Greystone.

What follows is a portion of a study whose aim was to describe Greystone Spanish Immersion School (K-5) in much the same way Salomone (1989) describes Glenwood French immersion school, that is, in the words of its teachers. The growing body of research on teacher thinking (see Clark & Peterson, 1986) indicates a similarly growing interest in turning to collaborative approaches to investigating why teachers do what they do when they are most occupied with the act of teaching. Since 1976, this body of research has grown substantially (Clark and Peterson, 1986), but has not yet touched significantly on the field of foreign language teaching.

Teachers' actions have been analyzed according to a number of different schemes. Typically, teaching may be characterized as consisting of sets of routines, shaped by planning and experience, that alter only when circumstances demand it (Clark & Yinger, 1977; Doyle, 1979; Shavelson & Stern, 1981:482). Indeed, Salomone's findings were relatively consistent with these views. The teachers she observed relied on carefully orchestrated routine to maximize classroom discipline and thereby, in their view, learning opportunities.

Inviting the collaboration of teachers, the research subjects, invites a great deal of unpredictability. Indeed, basic tenets of qualitative research demand willingness, on the part of the researcher, for information and impressions to develop unhampered by prior conceptions; at least, one acknowledges this bias in the process of observation (Lincoln & Guba, 1985). In the course of this study, the information developed primarily from the words and observations of teachers describing themselves. They spoke of general knowledge they had of teaching—their background and philosophies—and they were given the opportunity to reflect on their teaching as they watched themselves on videotape. Here, naturally, one encounters a phenomenon that Barer-Stein (1987) describes as the 'Paradox of Involvement':

> The more profound the Involving, the more deeply that Interest has become internalized and an inextricable part of oneself, the more it threads its way with the common, habitual daily activities of the individual. ...This is like saying, 'The better you know something the less you are aware of knowing it' (p. 101).

Breaking through teachers' automatic assumptions about their own behaviors can be a challenge. The process of extracting 'submerged' knowledge from beneath the seduction of 'superficial' knowledge (Barer-Stein, 1987) may be less than smooth; certainly, less than rapid. Rather, this mode of research necessitates a gradual formulation of teachers' realities as they themselves reveal it: in their words, in their actions, in the environment they establish for their work. That is, a steady reappraisal of all observations eventually exposes richer layers of meaning. This process is collaborative; its result is multilayered. Connelly & Clandinin (1990) carry the work of narrative inquiry such as this into the genre of story-telling resulting from 'negotiation of a shared narrative unity', underscoring the collaborative effort that constructs a given reality.

The observations and comments that follow are therefore merely preliminary attempts at describing the reality of a Spanish Immersion Elementary School. They reflect some consistency already with Salomone's findings, chiefly that these teachers are, first and foremost, elementary school teachers—not foreign-language teachers. Their primary concern is for the 'people' (one teacher's usual term for her students) that they teach. Overall, Salomone's provocative findings in the French Immersion Elementary School, located in the same midwestern city as this Spanish immersion school, suggest that much is to be discovered, and little to be assumed, about its Spanish counterpart. It was felt that a similar investigation of the Spanish immersion school might provide interesting additional insights, since the two schools, although sharing a common mission, are quite distinct.

Greystone, for instance, did not at first enjoy the overwhelming acceptance of its French sister school, partly because of its location in a lower-income neighborhood. Enrollment during the first year was complicated by a high percentage of students who applied for space simply because of the school's convenience to their neighborhood; that is, students and their parents had little genuine interest in the linguistic goals of the reorganized school. As a result, teachers tend to feel that the school is only now, three years later, beginning to show its true capability of producing bilingually competent and highly motivated students.

Furthermore, the atmosphere within Greystone is remarkably warm and lively, in contrast to the controlled, European-style ambience of its French sister. The school retains a singularly welcoming ambience of which the principal is openly proud:

> Greystone has something that most schools don't have, and that's a very warm atmosphere. Many people have commented that when they walked in the door they could actually feel... the warmth that is in the building. The love that the teachers have for the children, and that the children have for the teachers. It's just like a home away from home.

Greystone's beige brick exterior belies the liveliness of the interior. The color and brightness immediately impress the visitor; the walls here display more than simple ABCs. The inside front doors are wrapped with colorful paper in a South American motif and a pennant announces a bright 'Bienvenido' to the visitor. Greystone faculty and students have made sure that every inch of the building betrays the muticultural purpose of the instruction that takes place there. From the Spanish signs announcing the location of the fire extinguisher or the boys' bathroom to the hand-lettered 'Matrícula de Honor' [Honor Roll], the entire school 'speaks' Spanish. In the gym, which doubles as the cafeteria, national flags of the world's Spanish-speaking countries decorate the walls and are suspended from the ceiling. A three-paneled mural, painted by one of the teachers, displays a colorful and complex montage of salient aspects of Hispanic history, from El Greco to the Indians of the New World. The principal's office is richly decorated with woven and painted samples of Hispanic art. In one of the kindergarten rooms piñatas dance overhead. And everywhere, photographs and maps of the Hispanic world can be seen: cathedrals in Spain, green terraces in Macchu Pichu, rolling waves of the Cantabrian Sea.

Greystone does, of course, share its basic structure and method with the French immersion school with regard to the process and timing of immersion. Nonetheless, these two schools appear to have developed distinct personalities, and the descriptive nature of this study was intended to explore the unique nature of Greystone.

Requests were made of six of the teachers and positive responses received from five; of these, four contributed to the final study (one teacher returned to Puerto Rico during the study and so data collection could not be completed). Of these, the comments and observations of three are included here. Like Salomone's, this study maintained a naturalistic design and developed along the lines of 'teacher thinking' as characterized by Clark and others (see Clark & Peterson, 1986 for a comprehensive listing). To begin, a 'structured interview' elicited basic information from the teachers involved; the questions were provided to the teachers in advance, in response to their discomfort with 'not knowing what to expect'. Nonetheless, the interviews tended to expand into unplanned areas once the teachers became comfortable with the interview process, the interviewer, and the equipment on hand recording the conversation on both audio- and videotape. Teachers proved willing to provide information not only about themselves but about the school, their students, and their colleagues. Indeed, the warmth described by the principal carried through during all of the observation and interview portions of the present study.

A second interview, the 'stimulated recall' or element of reflection, allowed each teacher to comment on videotaped portions of her class. A common response to this session was that these tapes reflected, in effect, only one brief 'snapshot' of a classroom: a fair statement of an inherent limitation of the study. This restriction notwithstanding, the insight these teachers provide regarding their own teaching may serve to broaden the current understanding of the complex process of immersion teaching.

Preliminary analysis of both the informational interviews and the recall interviews reveals that teachers commented consistently on the use of routine in their classrooms. This fact alone coincides neatly with Salomone's study. Furthermore, teachers showed a pronounced concern for the self-esteem of their students, alongside a need to make decisions about discipline that would not discourage students from expressing themselves but would permit maximum attention on tasks. Such themes, and others, as they emerge from a thorough analysis of these interviews, will help to sketch a complete picture of a Spanish immersion school at work and encourage further investigation with teachers elsewhere.

Since a study of teacher thinking relies chiefly on teachers' observations of their own teaching, it is best, at this point, to return once again to the classroom where Barbara has moved from the window to the calendar, and permit Barbara herself to comment on her actions.

Later, she recalls this morning's lesson well. She seems to take for granted that her 'warm-up', as she calls it, is an excellent beginning for the busy day ahead. 'They are reviewing everything they are supposed to learn in the second grade', she explains. 'The ordinal numbers, days of the week, days of the month. Some language, some math: each opportunity to use the language'.

In the classroom, Barbara speaks quickly, in a style characteristically rapid that is recognized by her colleagues. Another teacher in the building acknowledges that, at the beginning of the school year, the children seem a bit awed by Barbara's rush of Spanish, despite their first two years' experience. But, adds the colleague, that's what the immersion experience is about. She notes: 'I don't think [teachers] should speak slower or faster than they normally would. They just need to be themselves'.

In Barbara's class the students volunteer comments and responses without being coached or prodded; they are accustomed to these mornings of counting, describing, listening, and speaking in Spanish. They appear relaxed and comfortable with the routine.

The other teacher continues:

> I know when children have gone to second grade that I had in first grade and they go to Sra Cano's room, well, Sra Cano is from Mexico; she speaks very, very fast. And at first, the first couple of weeks, I had one of my [former students'] parents tell me that she [the child] had no idea what Sra Cano was saying. And I said, 'Let her hang in there, she'll catch on', well, now that child has no problem. You know, why should Sra Cano change who and what she is to accommodate the children?'

When this immersion school began, the teachers agreed that the mission of the school must include inculcating a tolerance for diversity. The diversity of spoken Spanish within the school itself practically demanded this recognition. The numerous dialects themselves comprise a portion of what the teachers and principal proudly recognize as 'culture'.

One of the kindergarten teachers comments on the necessity for this tolerance:

When they leave my room, they're going to have a certain vocabulary for certain things... Just like, you know, why should I use the word 'café' [brown] if it doesn't feel comfortable and natural to me, because they're using it at other grade levels? You know, why should I change to fit someone else's mold or perception? When they go to [the next grade] and Sra Buendia says 'la guagua' for bus, that's what they pick up over there, but who am I to say, 'Hey, *la guagua* es feo, no digas eso'. ['Guagua is ugly, don't say that'.] That's what they use [where she comes from]. So, you know, the children learn to adjust... It's not just that [the students] are learning Spanish, but that they're picking up different cultures.

In her classroom, Barbara is recognizing the 'Estrella del Día': The Star of the Day. This activity honors one student each week (all students are eventually 'the star') by focusing questions on that student. It is Keisha's day today, and now the conversation focuses on her.

'¿Qué le gusta a Keisha [What does Keisha like]?' asks Barbara, and the girl's fellow students begin to recall, out loud, in Spanish, the things they know Keisha likes. They describe Keisha and Barbara supplies the word they seem to be looking for: 'aplicada' [applied, industrious]. Later, Barbara notes that she has never taught that word deliberately; 'it just came to my mind, because they really like Keisha'.

It is already a quarter after nine and now the class moves on to a brief language exercise. Barbara rapidly writes on the blackboard, '/valiente el elefante fue muy. /' and four other scrambled sentences. She admonishes them (in Spanish) not merely to write the correct sentence, but to 'think, only think it!' She walks to the back of the classroom and works with the children from that vantage point, watching the board, watching their heads, while she counts attendance and hot-lunch orders.

Throughout this entire twenty minutes of class, Barbara has rarely stopped talking; the class is continually inundated with a constant barrage of Spanish to which the students appear to respond without hesitation. Admits Barbara:

I bombard them!... I have from nine o'clock to nine twenty-five. And in that time all this is happening here! Attendance, people who interrupt, the announcements, Pledge of Allegiance, all that... That time of day you have ten minutes if you can use it for language, and those ten minutes can be a lot of language.

Ultimately, Barbara reveals that this seemingly rapid and complex set of activities consists primarily of well-exercised routine activities. She comments:

I don't assign the students, you know, but all of them are supposed to listen to the news and then they come and say, 'Okay, we [heard the news]...we are at 47 [degrees] but will be at 50 something', so they are aware that the things are going to go up or down depending on the weather. But they listen to the news, they are waiting for it.

The morning glance at the weather provides for a continually changing set of information within the context of a predictable use of language. Moreover, anticipation of this regular activity encourages the students to prepare themselves by gathering the necessary information before coming to class each day. As Barbara herself admits, she does not overtly assign such preparation, but the routine itself invites the ongoing interest of the students. 'They like to be part of the whole thing', continues Barbara. 'Because if I give everything, all the information, they will be bored. So they are the ones providing the information'.

Adherence to routine, then, does not preclude cultivating students' independence. To the contrary, these predictable blocks of activity allow for lighter supervision of children working independently. Barbara, for example, relies on having established a routine of study- center use for mathematics, reading, and spelling that allows her to work intently on reading with a small group of students:

> We used to do most of this in the large [classroom] group, mostly because it was needed and their vocabulary was expanding... [But now] I feel confident that they can go by themselves and control their behavior and their time and apply themselves to the tasks to be able to finish in fifty minutes. That's enough; if they don't do their part, everything fails. So it won't depend just on me. It depends on them. And they are aware that they are an important part of the whole...

It is clear that Barbara relies on students' independence and responsibility, and that her careful orchestration of the day encourages both.

Part of Barbara's morning routine necessarily includes presentation of the daily schedule detailing the location of each small group as it rotates from one study center to the next: from math, to spelling, to reading. Although Barbara is now confident that the students will work quietly and industriously together, the initial difficulty, she admits, was with the schedule itself:

> See, they weren't able to follow a chart like that [at first]... At the beginning, they were confused. Now they are becoming proficient. That takes practice. But it's a practice that is needed, because they're supposed to know where to go. When I'm at the reading table, I'm not going to stop, and I want to devote all my time to that group, and [the

others] are supposed to be not [doing busywork] but busy in the sense [of] doing something important.

In other words, establishing the routine necessitated imparting certain skills—i.e. how to read a time chart—and the language associated with it. A routine, then, is not gratuitous administrative management, but a linguistically-rich learning event in itself.

Down the hall in the kindergarten classroom, practiced routines are underway even before the school day officially begins. Maureen, one of the school's two kindergarten teachers, explains the morning activity:

> Generally, I set up the morning, the beginning of the morning, with something for the kids to do, so that when they straggle in between twenty of nine and 9:05...I generally have something on the tables for them to do, with written instructions on the board. And I've done that since the beginning. Believe it or not. At the beginning I would just put a ditto [on the tables] and I would put a color word, then say a word, and they had to figure out what the color word meant, and color it that way... I have a color chart on the board... So I start off the day with something that I think is reasonably useful and challenging, and they help each other if they haven't learned to read it. This week, I started putting up a picture that says 'camello' on the picture. 'El camello es...amarillo'. And I didn't say a word, and I heard little children going, 'El camello es...amarillo'. ...And they did it. That's the beginning of the day.

Again, this simple before-school routine is not mere busywork:

> I start it off with something that's independent and hopefully that challenges them a little bit... It isn't free play. ...I mean, it may look a little chaotic, but if you came in here you'd see kids sitting at this table writing, or sitting on the floor reading, and then when I tell them that we're ready to go, they come back to the table. So that gives the slow ones a chance to finish, and the fast ones a chance to do something creative on their own, independent.

Once the school bell has rung, Maureen's class is ready for a 'block' of language development. In fact, Maureen delineates the day by such blocks:

> I like to work in blocks. I like to know that I'm going to work till this time and then we're going to go to gym, or till this time and go to the bathroom. It just sort of makes a natural break. And I tend to like that, just part of my style.

This initial block lasts twenty minutes, 'and the reason it's twenty minutes is we all signed up for bathroom break and I got 9:25!' confesses

Maureen. 'So I try to do something that's a twenty-minute lesson that works'.

One such lesson has the students talk about feelings and practice the basic conversational gambit, '¿Cómo estás?' The children are seated at three large tables and Maureen stands in front of the class. She begins by asking the children how they feel, then holds up flashcards with sketched faces and asks the children,

'¿Cómo estás?'

'¡Triste! [Sad!]' they shout, or '¡Enfermo! [Sick!]' according to the sketch.

Maureen then slowly pulls one card out of the bundle, intentionally building suspense as she looks at it, then holds it behind her back. She frowns and her brows knit.

'¡Enojada! [Angry!]' shout most of the children, the remainder joining in as the answer becomes clear. After acting out three of these, Maureen looks around at the tables, again building suspense; the children wiggle and laugh. At last, she calls on one student, who joins her at the front of the class. She shows the picture only to that child, who acts out the emotion depicted on the card. As the other children guess which it is, the classroom becomes noisy with shrieks of laughter and yelled-out guesses.

Maureen uses this first block to introduce new vocabulary, such as that required by the local 'Course of Study' for health instruction; one week she concentrated on 'community helpers'. She finds that 'it's just a nice little block of time when I can play games with them or set up language patterns that I want them to learn'.

When they return from their bathroom break the children file automatically to the 'alfombra', the carpet, at the back of the classroom. Maureen greets them as they choose their places. She is wearing a name-tag sized piece of paper pinned to the front of her blue jump suit, as she does everyday; today, the tag bears a capital 'J' and a small 'j'. This is the letter of the day; later, the children will practice writing the letter and words that begin with that letter.

In order to quiet the children, Maureen stands patiently on the colorful carpet and looks around to find children who have settled down.

'Gracias a.... Elizabeth', she says in a calm voice, 'y gracias a'....—here she looks around some more—'a Gary'... By naming those who display behaviors she is waiting for, she calls attention to desirable behavior. 'My option is to scream and yell until they sit down', explains Maureen. 'I do it this way, which is a lot less energy for me'.

Still standing on the carpet, she continues to reinforce the behavior she wants:

'Espero... [I'm waiting]', she warns, her voice becoming sterner, 'hasta que estén listos. Hasta que todos estén como... [until you are ready. Until all of you are like...]' and she looks around again for an example of good behavior, 'Howard'.

Maureen spends almost two minutes settling the children onto the carpet, naming well-behaved students in a calm litany until almost all are paying attention. 'I'm trying to get them together in line', she recalls. 'It sounds funny, but when we need to count the kids, if they're not in line, they can't count [themselves]. I can't count [them]'.

Here, she is anticipating portions of the learning block about to take place. Although it, too, involves a routine exercise in language, it incorporates administrative necessities such as taking attendance. Like Barbara, Maureen tries to avoid devoting exclusive time to such duties but attempts to carry them out along with the lesson at hand.

'Espero [I'm waiting]!' announces Maureen. '¡Estoy lista [I'm ready]!'

Finally all the children are arranged in satisfactory, although still somewhat loose, order on the carpet and Maureen compliments them:

'Muy bien. Excelente'.

She then takes her seat before the bulletin board. It is decorated with a large calendar of the month, each day represented by a separate, removable piece of paper. She removes today's date from the row of remaining days at the margin of the calendar, and pins it in place. Above the calendar are large, cut-out block letters: ?QUE DIA ES HOY? [WHAT DAY IS IT?]

Pointing to the day, Maureen leads the children in a choral recitation:

Hoy es jueves el veinticinco de... [Today is Thursday, the twenty-fifth of...].

One child loudly insists that it is still 'noviembre' rather than 'enero' [January]. When a misunderstanding such as this occurs, Maureen prefers not to correct overtly:

First of all, you count on peer pressure. That's usually [construed as] negative, but here it's, you know... Four people [do what you want] so they pick it up from each other... It's peer leadership.

In this case, Maureen remedies the error by consulting the class, who repeat the correct month. At the same time, another child interrupts: 'Está lloviendo [it's raining]'. 'Sí', agrees Maureen, reaching behind her for a stack of laminated tagboard labels displaying the different days of the week. Later, she comments on the continuous interruptions by the children:

They have this routine down so pat that they run the show now. They know they're going to tell me what the weather's all about, and I don't want to squelch them because that's what it's all about.

Nonetheless, before coming to the weather, Maureen wants to complete the calendar activity. One by one she holds up the days of the week and asks individual students,

'¿Qué dice [What does this say]?'

Each answers correctly until she reaches Eric, who is stumped by 'jueves [Thursday]'. Maureen turns to point to the large calendar. 'Lunes [Monday]', she begins, and then Eric takes over: 'Martes, miércoles.... jueves!'

I'm doing this because I'm trying to make those sight words, and out of the nineteen kids I would say that fourteen can read them. Out of order, on sight... They write them, they play with them and you know, they love them.. It's a source of things that they get good at, too, and they can use it as a toy. So that's why I do it. It also shows me who knows. A couple of times what I've done is I've hidden the day—like, today is Thursday, I would have hidden Thursday. I'll go all the way around the class and after about eight students [have read the labels], somebody will say, 'She's tricking us!' They realize that I have hidden that day. And again that's also good, that's good memory... I may start doing it with the months of the year.

Maureen gives Eric a big smile and hands him the label. He walks to the calendar to fasten it above the month. The remaining children take advantage of the break to begin speaking with each other, and Maureen looks at them with a frown, her arms crossed sternly. Immediately the children are quiet again.

'Vamos a contar los días hasta hoy [Let's count the days up to today]', she instructs.

'Can we count past hoy?' asks one of the more precocious students in the class.

'Hasta hoy', repeats Maureen calmly, and calls on another student to come to the calendar and lead the count. She and the class monitor him as he quickly, breathlessly, counts to the twenty-fifth. Maureen looks at the children on the carpet and smiles her approval of a good job of counting.

At growing signs of restlessness, Maureen says, in a slightly louder voice,

'Quiero oírlos cantar hoy [I want to hear you sing today]'.

Immediately she begins singing their daily weather song:

'¿Qué tiempo hace? Hace frío [How is the weather? It's cold]'...

Soon all the children have joined in for the rest of the song, which recites all the weather conditions they use in their morning reports: rain, snow, clouds, sun, heat, cold, wind. From here, the class moves smoothly to the writing of the day's weather report on the blackboard immediately to the left of the calendar.

Singing about the weather does more than reinforce or review vocabulary for this activity; Maureen often uses song as a control tactic as well. Throughout this activity block, some of the children periodically become restless, talking out of turn and walking around. Maureen has a number of strategies for coping with the natural fidgetiness of five-year-olds. She may sit or stand calmly, arms crossed, waiting; she may speak a child's name sternly; or she may again call attention to a child demonstrating the proper behavior. At other times, when it seems apparent their energy level is getting the better of them, she simply launches into song. Maureen describes this preferred tactic:

> When I start singing like that I'm trying to get them all together, and I'm not a very intimidating person and so there are certain things that I do that may not be good enough to try and get them together. In other words, all on the same wavelength, at the same time, looking at me, let's go together. Because otherwise I ...try not to teach them if somebody's looking here, somebody's looking there... Because it's, who knows what's going in. So these are some things that I do just to try and get them all on the same tune, same wavelength.

After the activities on the carpet have concluded, usually with a round of singing, it is time to return to the tables. Again, Maureen is working in blocks, and these transitions make it easy for her to send one or two children to work with learning specialists elsewhere in the building:

> I send three kids who are reading up to [the reading specialist] and I do that whenever, you know, it's a natural break here [for them] to go over there, that's a natural time for them to go up. I don't have to point out to everybody else that these kids are going to reading. They just sort of flow out.

Maureen's 'blocks' of activities reflect her natural organization according to routines that allow both predictable opportunities for language use as well as easy transitions that permit flexibility. Blocks of activity may be interchanged, lengthened, shortened, or eliminated; Maureen looks for 'natural' breaking points to make transitions:

> I don't like to watch the clock. We're a lot more self- contained, so if...things are wonderful we go for it and if they're not wonderful you stop and you go somewhere else.

The other kindergarten class at Greystone is Julie's responsibility. In structuring her day, she responds to concerns similar to those of Maureen. Above all, she sounds concerned about the ability of the children to persevere through a rigorous day of learning and language absorption:

By 2:00, I'd say the children are ready to tune me out. So we sometimes have another free time or a cut-and-paste activity or something that they don't really have to think about, something that they can relax and do. Then... around 2:30 we go outside and play...then we get ready to go home. And we have to always keep in mind that, you know, they have been here all day and it is a hard day for them because it's a second language.

Interestingly, later in the same interview, Julie puts less blame on the immersion system:

The component is that it's such a long day, that's what makes them so tired....They would be just as tired in a monolingual school.

Julie, too, relies on a clear set of routines to minimize trauma for teacher and students:

Right off the bat, first day, they begin learning that there's routine. 'There's a way that Sra. McCormick wants me to do something and that's the way I need to do it'.

Routines in Julie's classroom extend beyond supervising sets of activities; she adamantly instills expectations of individual behavior in the children. Having grown up bilingually herself, she comments regularly on her concern for each child's ability to keep his attention on the work at hand and bases her approach on this concern:

The bottom line: In immersion learning, these children can't afford to look out the window, can't afford to stop and play with their shoes; they've got to be keyed into me, one hundred per cent of the time. Because if they aren't completely on me one hundred per cent of the time, they'll miss it. They are going to miss it. That's why I insist, when I'm going to explain something [here she snaps her fingers]—Hey, you're not looking at me, and I go like this. You're not listening to me. That's why when we're passing out papers or I'm explaining something up at the board, I say, 'Look at me with your hands on your knees'. If their hands are on their knees they're not going to be playing with a piece of paper, they're not going to be touching the person next to them, they're not going to have anything in their hands. And they have to look at the board because they have nothing else to do. They have to look at me.

Whether due to immersion or to school stress, these demands also create a concomitant need for completely independent playtime for the kindergartners. She notes: 'By the same token, when it's time, Well hey! "You play how you want". Because it's their time'.

In fact, during free time in Julie's classroom, the noise level rises virtually uninhibited, and Julie attends to her own work while the children interact as they wish. Only if activities become overly energetic or noisy will she intervene.

> That's their time! And as long as they're not running or hitting each other, I pretty much let them do what they do, because, again, they need to get a lot of this out. They need to release a lot of their energy. So as long as they're playing and no one is being hurt, it's okay. But when I really feel that they need to sit and listen, that's what I want them to do.... They know what to expect from me all the time. And they know what I expect from them, which is just as important.

Her insistence on the need to command absolute attention arises repeatedly. As she watches herself on videotape, Julie remembers what was on her mind during the lesson: the fact that one of her students, due to absenteeism, may not be able to focus to the degree she considers vital:

> This little boy here, he has a hard time staying on track. Also, at the point of this video, he had missed fifteen and a half school days. And if you're missing school you're not going to get the language. They're not getting the language at home, so they have to be at school to get the language. And the more they're not at school—he has a real big problem with absenteeism—the more he's going to tune me out because he has been missing, missing and less and less of what I say is making any sense to him.

In verbalizing her thoughts about this particular child, Julie demonstrates her conviction about the role she plays in the lives and minds of the children she teaches. She is the sole source of their Spanish input; it is her duty to see to it they spend their time on task, absorbing as much as possible. As long as she controls the environment, the rest happens naturally:

> The children come in real excited, they want to do this. And it is so effortless for them to pick it up. They're just little sponges. So there's nothing to it for them. You know, they're eager to learn more and say more.

Still, when Julie was given the opportunity to comment on transcripts of her reflections, she expressed a concern that she might be perceived 'as an ogre'. She felt that her words, taken out of the context of her classroom, give an impression of a harsh, almost punitive approach to discipline. Yet she herself admits, during the interview, to having a positive relationship with the children:

> I don't know; I have maybe parental, maternalistic feelings... toward my children, and it makes me feel good. ...I don't think my style is bad for the children. I know it seems kind of strict and maybe someone else would view it as harsh. You can see for yourself I get many unsolicited hugs and kisses throughout the day. Never do I say, you know, 'It's hugging time, come and give me a hug'. No! It comes from within, from all of them, even from little Beau, who I probably scold the most!

Whereas Julie makes explicit demands on the children about their behavior, Maureen is uncomfortable with this role:

> I wish they had self-discipline! It's important, and I think that's another one of my shortcomings, that it doesn't happen real easily. I don't like them to be little soldiers. I'm uncomfortable and you know, I can't, when I finally get them quiet... But I think that the interaction [during discipline] is good for them, too. ...I think that discipline is a real hard number. There are certain kids that want to please you, and that isn't the point. They should want to please themselves, you know, but how do you get that across?

She, too, ties the importance for classroom control to the need for attention to the foreign language:

> It's necessary. ...It is important. That's another thing about learning [in] a second language, that they tend to focus more because they're going to miss something if they don't.

Yet the children themselves are not, according to Maureen, aware of this connection; therefore, it is her job to keep them on task:

> I don't think that they're aware of [the need to focus]. I think it just happens. I don't think they're aware of it; it's just self-preservation. Because basically they don't seem to tune me out. You can tell when they're tuning me out, you know they're looking out somewhere else and they don't tend to do that.

Out of a high degree of sympathy for the task their students face in acquiring regular content through the medium of a foreign language, neither Julie nor Maureen wishes to discourage her students by punishing them, even inadvertently. Julie's explicit expectations of behavior intend to obviate this, or at least make disciplinary actions predictable and regular, rather than unexpected and personal. Maureen utilizes a variety of tactics that reflect her unwillingness to administer discipline outright. She focuses attention on students manifesting 'proper' behavior; she starts up a song to bring everyone's attention back to the group.

During the recall, she points out an additional tactic as well. What at first looks like a purely pedagogical device turns out to reflect her ongoing awareness that a child may be temporarily 'tuning out'. While one child reads aloud the writing on the blackboard, Maureen 'tracks' the words by pointing with her finger:

> I do it on purpose. I generally touch the first letter and not the whole word... It keeps the other kids who aren't reading, on my finger. She [the student shown on the tape] doesn't need me to do that, she could do that, but it keeps the other kids, I think, with me. It's what I think, not what I know...You know, it seems to me that if somebody is looking, like Emily, is looking this way and then all of a sudden she decides she's interested, she's going to know where we are. And that gives her a chance. I'm not going to punish her because she doesn't know where I am... Kristen [who's reading] doesn't need it, and any other kid that would raise his hand and ask to read wouldn't need it, but he knows where he is. So, that's why I do it.

In other words, Maureen recognizes that it is a natural occurrence for a child's attention to wander, just as Julie recognizes the need for a completely unrestricted play time that allows the children to 'get it out of their system'. Once again, Maureen is attending to discipline without needing to apply punitive *post-hoc* measures.

Similarly, in the second grade classroom, Barbara strives to accept all of her students' comments in a positive fashion, rather than seeking something more 'correct'. While conducting the morning weather review, for instance, Barbara notes that on the way to school she heard on the radio that it was warm enough to barbecue. She asks for the name of another season during which barbecues are normal. The students answer, 'Otoño!' [Autumn!] Barbara explains why she was happy with this unexpected response:

> Okay, at the beginning of the year it was Fall, so remember that winter followed the Fall and in their minds all those experiences, like Halloween, well, all of those things were related to the weather. So Spring is far away from their minds because it comes after Winter [and it is still Winter now]. To them it's closer. [The time for barbecues] can be Fall because they know they still barbecued [in the fall]...It's accurate, you would think of that, you do barbecue in Fall, too. So to me that's good. And I can let them know, yes, I do accept this, because we can do this in Fall, too. In fact we have [such] beautiful days that we want to stop the season! So that is that.

Not only can she justify the logic of the response she has received, but she generally insists on interpreting the students' utterances in this positive fashion:

> ...You try to accept more than reject. And if you say, 'No, that is wrong', they will stop. But you don't know when that light, that flame comes, you know?

Later in the same interview, she adds, 'It doesn't make any sense to condemn or criticize'.

Like Maureen with her various methods, and Julie with her early instilling of expected behaviors, Barbara prefers to administer classroom control preventively. Of course, she is able to work with her second graders at a higher level of language and behavior. Having instituted a fairly regular schedule of autonomous study via the study centers she has created, she communicates her trust of the students, and this allows her to work more intently with small groups. In other words, her approach to discipline reflects an interest in the ability of the group to function profitably. She feels that the students are aware of this intent and cooperate well.

By the same token, these teachers are loath to correct students' language errors. This aversion is consistent with their reluctance to do anything less than (in Barbara's words, again) 'accept...not reject', and to prefer encouraging good behavior to punishing bad. Rather than correct errors, then, they strongly prefer to model correct forms.

Maureen describes a typical instance:

> Kristen [made such an error] today, I'm trying to remember, and I just sort of whispered in her ear the right way to do it. And that wasn't, I don't know, I think I was trying to be, well, I was trying not to put her down.

Julie engages the students in a daily activity that allows her time to model their own language efforts back to them individually. After reading a simple story (that she and Maureen have written together), she asks the children to draw a picture about themselves in the story. She calls them to her desk one at a time, where they describe the picture:

> ...All I'm doing is writing what they say. And another thing I'm doing is I'm modelling the correct way to say the response. ...See, they don't always say it grammatically correct and I'm modelling it back.

She also conducts this activity with the whole group, as an introduction to the writing exercise. At that time, she will write the child's response on the easel for the class to see. Each child's response is praised copiously by her.

As the videotape continues to play back this activity, Julie reflects on a particular interaction:

Complete sentence. No problem. And I'm deliberately writing it slow and I'm repeating it for a reason, as a model, so the other children can hear what's going on. And as you can see I am letting them all hear the response out loud so they can all hear it. And to give them all the opportunity to use the language.

Indeed, she speaks quite slowly as she repeats the child's response and records it. 'And in here, you hear no talking', Julie comments. 'It's quiet. They're all learning'. The room is hushed as Julie conducts this lesson. 'That's my style', she continues. 'In work time it's work time; in play time, it's play time'. Again, she has reiterated her system of expectations for the students' ongoing behavior.

The scene repeats itself with another child. This time, Julie comments on her habit of repeating, slowly, clearly, and correctly, precisely what the child has said:

Because we never want to say, 'Oh, no, that's wrong, this is how you say it'. We'd rather just model it back the correct way to say it. Because once you start telling children, 'Oh, that's wrong, gotta say it like this, that's wrong!' Then everything they say [they will be afraid] is wrong.

In kindergarten, Julie and Maureen do not expect perfect Spanish. Rather, they appear to prefer to encourage the uninhibited drive for self-expression that motivates these young students to speak freely, whether in English, Spanish, or a combination. When Julie reflects on another such scene, she is clearly proud of the child's courage:

What they're doing here is they're sharing their story. So it's all voluntary. I don't force them to come up and read. But if they want to read, they do. He just said 'Mi' [i.e. instead of 'Yo']. I asked who else wanted to read and he said 'Mi'. Yes [that's modelling]. See how shy and quiet he is? But I'm not saying, 'Oh, you can't read this, sit down'. I'm letting him come up and have his chance.

On the tape, Julie's voice is quite clear. '¡Un carro! ¡Muy bien!'

'He drew a car', Julie continues reflecting. 'I'm praising him for what he has done. It takes a lot of guts to come up and do that. And you can hear, they're on the carpet, you can't hear anything'. Again, she is proud of their attending to her expectations.

Their overriding concern for the welfare of their students tempers Julie's and Maureen's intentions to instill Spanish. Both become emotional when discussing this priority. Both independently use the example of fire drills to illustrate.

Julie: How could I *possibly* explain a fire drill and what it's all about, and what we're supposed to do, in Spanish? And feel comfortable that the children knew what I was doing? There's absolutely no way... What if we're discussing a fire drill and they don't understand it, then what if there's a fire? If there really is a fire?

Maureen: I'm probably not supposed to speak English at all. But some things are dangerous. When it was a fire drill and they went out there and they got in that line, if I didn't come back in here and tell them what they just did, what good is it?

Obviously, speaking Spanish is the mission of the school; the safety and general welfare of the students, however, appear to be among the primary concerns of the teachers, taking precedence over language acquisition and accuracy. These teachers therefore face a daily task of honoring both directives. Early development of workable routines appears to assist the teachers in satisfying both goals.

The categories of routine, discipline, self-esteem, and language modelling coincide, at this stage of analysis, with Salomone's findings, even without quantitative assessment of frequency and hierarchy. Nonetheless, even coincident findings must be considered within their context; that is, the complex reality of Greystone Elementary School itself. Final analysis, therefore, depends on furthering the collaboration between researcher, subjects, and environment in a continual reassessment of how these aspects coordinate—how they 'tell their story' together.

Part 2:
Studies of Immersion Classrooms

3 Learning Through Drama in the Immersion Classroom

DEBORAH WILBURN

Introduction

One of the main characteristics of teachers in an immersion setting is their seemingly natural ability to create a world for second language learning based on gesturing, body language, and exaggeration (Salomone, this volume). The techniques used for creating and enhancing such a world—drama—are the focus of this chapter. The effects of drama as a tool for immersion language learning are substantiated herein.

Drama extends beyond that which teachers bring in the way of outward manifestations. It includes how teachers build on their existing classroom practices by incorporating the new dimensions of learning offered by drama. One dimension focuses on the idea of empowering children with their own learning through the teacher's subtle manipulation of the unfolding drama. Another aspect is that drama offers a context for actively using language as a means to an end rather than practicing language as in vocabulary and grammar drills. Drama, then, as a learning tool, draws on content from across the curriculum, instilling a deep sense of understanding by involving children emotionally with the content. Third, drama seeks to build social competence and confidence amongst participants through purposeful work with others. Finally, it promotes individual responsibility to the group effort and a willingness to accept and respect the ideas of others.

This chapter will begin with a discussion of the theoretical assumptions from first and second language acquisition research that undergird the use of drama in the immersion classroom. Previous texts on the incorporation of drama techniques in second language settings will then be reviewed, as well as guides to drama in the classroom from first language research.

Next, a description of the setting and procedures for this examination of drama in language immersion will be chronicled. Having established a conceptual framework for the reader, a discussion of emerging views from this study and the analysis of these views will ensue. The chapter will conclude with suggestions for further research.

The Use of Drama in Educational Contexts

Second language acquisition research is replete with the ideas of comprehensible input (Krashen, 1985a), comprehensible output (Swain, 1985), and negotiation of meaning through interaction (Long, 1981). Drama provides an arena for the practical application of many of these theories. Each dramatic context necessitates different kinds of language—interactional here, heuristic there—as well as various styles and registers. As a drama unfolds, many of the seven language functions identified by Halliday (1973) come into play, allowing participants to experience language purposefully in meaningful situations to accomplish a variety of tasks.

As a technique, drama is compatible with the whole language philosophy so prevalent in current language arts programs (Altwerger, Edelsky & Flores 1987). Language, oral and written, is considered to be a tool for making sense of the world. There is no dividing line between reading, discussion, listening, and writing time in the whole language classroom. Rather, one activity flows naturally to the next. In solving the problems put forth in drama, it is often necessary for the participants to consult books, write letters, draw pictures, and discuss plans. The need for a variety of media arises intrinsically as the drama progresses.

Although the participants in a drama are creating the story together, drama is more concerned with a thorough understanding of the present situation rather than moving the story forward as in a narrative. The problem is attacked using a variety of media at a rather slow pace resulting in factual knowledge as well as a true sense of ownership for the eventual understanding reached. One of the primary purposes of drama is to promote reflection in learning.

Incorporating drama into a second language setting is by no means a new idea. Smith (1984) provides a practical guide for adult second language learners working through simulations or full-fledged play productions. Smith draws parallels between how actors prepare for a part through observation, character study, verbal and nonverbal modifications, and how astute language learners engaging in similar behaviors increase their potential for linguistic and sociolinguistic competence. Smith's conception of the teacher's role is analogous to that of the director on Broadway: he provides freedom with direction, introduces elements for rehearsal, stops and starts the rehearsal to call attention to certain linguistic or nonlinguistic features, and prescribes that his actors (students) write down elements under discussion for future reflection.

McRae (1985) advocates using authentic dramatic texts in teaching English to adult second language learners. His text is prescriptive in nature, offering advice concerning the teacher's role, how and when to lead participants to a semi-autonomous state of learning, and what the teacher should focus upon and expand upon to further curiosity and exploration about a given theme. McRae's theoretical conception of drama rests on the premise that as students experience and work through new situations, both their linguistic competence and their knowledge of the world will increase, leading to a deeper understanding of the human condition. In this respect, his underlying philosophy of learning reflects a great belief in ownership as a means of arriving at true understanding.

Di Pietro (1987) suggests using scenarios sequenced by interactive complexity to provide students with a context that necessitates meaningful, real-life negotiation and interaction. The methodology requires adherence to a three-phase lesson: rehearsal, performance, and debriefing. With beginning language learners, rehearsal and performance are often combined. Scenarios have been used in ESL and FL settings with subject matter suitably adjusted for a variety of age levels. The technique stresses fluency over accuracy and production as a means to comprehension. Di Pietro views literacy development as flowing from the discussion and enactment of the scenario. Students write about what they have experienced first-hand, from a common pool of understanding. Readings are chosen which reflect the same themes evident in the scenarios.

First language literature concerning drama offers many of the same kinds of teaching strategies. Bolton (1979) provides a theoretical framework for successful drama activities in the classroom. A classification of various drama techniques along with a discussion of dramatic structures and elements necessary to ensure success are given.

Neelands (1984) provides a concise review of the theoretical assumptions for incorporating drama in the classroom along with a practical guide for its implementation. Whether expanding upon an idea from an authentic text or creating a drama together in the classroom based upon a task conceived by the teacher, this type of drama evolves out of two important childhood learning modes: storying and direct experience. By asking participants questions which necessitate careful consideration of possible options, the teacher leads children in their meaning-making without imposing his/her own adult attitudes on the subject. As with other forms of drama, the context necessitates the medium and the style of language.

However, unlike other dramatic techniques, Neeland's conception is quite flexible in nature. The drama may be stopped and started as needed either in or out of role to evaluate the work or firm up understanding.

O'Neill & Lambert (1982) provide the most comprehensive treatment of the benefits of incorporating drama in the classroom. The authors list attractive, educational processes activated by drama. These include: inquiry, critical and constructive thought, problem-solving, skills of comparison, interpretation, judgment, and discrimination, and finally a desire to further learning and research.

For second language teachers, the contribution of drama to language learning provides the principal justification for its use. O'Neill & Lambert offer a theoretical explanation:

> One of the most positive contributions which drama makes to the curriculum is that it provides a facilitating atmosphere for many kinds of language use. Language is the cornerstone of the drama process...Drama can provide a powerful motivation to speech, and this speech does not occur in isolation but is embedded in context and situation where it has a crucial organizing function (p. 17).

Within educational drama, the teacher acts as a structural agent while leaving room for participants to influence the outcome of the activity. Therefore, the teacher begins by clearly defining for him/herself the aims, approaches, and boundaries to be used for each session. By building the drama around the theater elements of focus, tension, surprise, contrast, and symbolization, the teacher establishes the intrinsic structure of the drama. Once the activity is underway, the teacher draws upon a repertoire of strategies to respond to developments within the drama. Working in drama, the language of both teachers and participants creates and controls the situation, regulates the activity, defines the roles, and binds the group together (O'Neill & Lambert, 1983).

In appraising the language capabilities of individual students engaged in drama, teachers are cognizant of categories of language in which learners should develop increasing competence. These categories include: (1) describing past experiences, (2) instructing and explaining, (3) logical reasoning, convincing, and persuading, and (4) planning, predicting, and deciding (O'Neill & Lambert, 1983). Documenting language samples from each student enables the teacher to chart the growth processes of language and, combined with other means of assessment typical in the classroom, provides a composite picture of the student's linguistic competence.

It is useful to compare and contrast the various terms often referred to which fall under the rubric of drama activities. Figure 3.1 lists and defines some of the techniques above. A glance at the table indicates that many of the descriptions of drama activities could easily define 'second language activities'. On reflection, it is easy to understand why, building on the dramatic acts central to FL teaching in general, and immersion teaching in particular (Salomone, this volume), drama in the formal sense of O'Neill, Lambert & Neelands was a logical choice of techniques to study in the immersion setting.

---

theatre arts: script provided. actors/students study roles to enact in culturally authentic ways. actors perfect body language, gestures, stress and intonation. use all senses to feel the role.

creative dramatics or dramatic play: the experience of pretending stressed. no reflection. little direction.

role play: students play someone else. told what to do and say. players know position of others. target language used to reinforce previously presented items from the syllabus. similar to a one episode drama but more focused, functional, and purposeful.

simulations: students play someone else. setting and position pre-determined by teacher or described on commercially prepared cards. players do not know each other's positions in the interaction. structured and controlled by reality. teacher as controller—keeps action moving.

scenarios: student plays self within framework of role. role specifies situational details but not position to be taken. interaction contains greater amount of uncertainty and dramatic tension than in role play. target language structures which emerge from the interaction determine the linguistic syllabus. rehearsal and debriefing conducted in L1 until linguistically competent. teacher as counselor in rehearsal, orchestrator in performance, discussion leader in debriefing.

drama: teacher in role. students have choice over setting, roles, why they're involved, direction drama will take. teacher sets problem or task. overall structure becomes intrinsic based on focus, tension, surprise, contrast, and symbolization. if...then orientation. has a form of its own like a story which evolves. can move in space and time, backwards and forwards. draws on world of imagination as well as content from across the curriculum. not bound by realism. focus is student/subject directed.

Figure 3.1 Terms and descriptions of drama activities

The Study

Setting

This study was conducted over an eight month period (August–March) in a Spanish immersion school. Greystone is part of a large urban school system in the Midwestern region of the United States. The school has been operating for three years and serves kindergarten through fifth grade students. Children from the immediate neighborhood as well as those chosen by lottery attend Greystone.

Participants

Three teachers from Greystone volunteered their classes for this study: Ana, a first grade teacher, Linda, a second grade teacher, and Maria, the fourth grade teacher. All three are bilingual Spanish/English speakers, the first two being of Hispanic origin. Moreover, they were educated in the United States and are familiar with elementary methods appropriate for American children.

Brett, a drama instructor from a large university near Greystone, worked with the three classes mentioned above while two research assistants from the university filmed the proceedings.

Procedures

Conducting ethnographic research such as this requires the trust and cooperation of the administration, staff, and students of the participating school. To this end, the visiting team (professor-in-charge of grant, two research assistants, drama instructor) was quite visible from the very beginning of the school year. On the first day of school, the professor-in-charge briefly explained the purpose of the researchers' work to the staff and administration. For the next six weeks, the researchers spent several days each week observing classes and chatting informally over lunch in an effort to establish a collaborative, mutually respectful relationship with the teachers. The presence of the researchers in the building also enabled the students to grow accustomed to the visitors and learn to 'ignore' them.

This preliminary stage was crucial to the success of our work for it surfaced that, even though the teachers were outwardly friendly, they had many questions as to the nature of our observation notes and our ulterior motives for watching them so closely. ('Were these people from the university actually here evaluating us?') It was decided to provide copies of the observation notes for the teachers after each visit to allay their fears. After this practice was implemented, the staff and principal visibly relaxed and provisions were made to begin the second stage of the research.

In October, Brett visited the school with the primary researcher acting as an interpreter and guide. They observed each classroom for approximately 10 minutes and then joined the teachers over lunch for an informal discussion.

Two teachers volunteered to work with Brett at that time: Ana, the first grade teacher, and Maria, the fourth grade teacher. The purpose of this early work was to generate discussion amongst the teachers concerning drama in the classroom and to provide the researchers with an opportunity to tape an actual immersion class using drama for a subsequent in-service with the entire faculty.

In November, Brett held an in-service for all of the teachers at Greystone during which he explained his background as an elementary teacher and his philosophy concerning drama. Excerpts from the work taped in the first and fourth grade classes served as concrete examples of the possibilities Brett offered to the staff for using drama. As in any good in-service, he actively involved the teachers in many drama-related activities. The proceedings were videotaped for future reference by the staff and the research team.

Time precluded all of the interested teachers from working with Brett. Only Linda, a second grade teacher, was added to the two original volunteers.

Over the course of the remaining five months, seventeen videotapes were recorded. The majority of the work was carried out with Ana, the first grade teacher. Four themes were fully explored with her students to produce a total of nine tapes. Linda's second grade class worked with two themes yielding three tapes. The remaining five tapes were produced with the help of Maria's fourth graders who focused on two themes.

Each session with Brett typically lasted about 1.5 hours. The teacher was given a role that required the students to respond to her in Spanish (i.e. the director of a Mexican zoo, a customs official, a suspect in an assassination attempt). Brett assumed roles where it was reasonable for him to speak English since he is not conversant in Spanish (i.e. a CIA man, a journalist from the United States, an emissary of one of the Three Wise Kings). During the early dramas, Brett retained much of the control—framing the problem, asking probing questions of the students, and deciding when to come out of the drama for reflection. As the teachers grew more and more comfortable working in the medium, they assumed greater responsibility for the management of the dramas.

Emerging Views

The purpose of this study was to arrive at an understanding of how emphasizing drama in an immersion setting affects classroom behaviors. Observing drama in action for eight months has led to some tentative conclusions in the areas of classroom discourse, language arts methodologies, and language across the curriculum. These are:

(1) Drama changes the nature of teacher talk and student discourse by enhancing the already meaningful context of immersion through the purposeful use of language.
(2) Working in drama complements the whole language approach to language arts in that the resolution of the task (see Prabhu, 1987; Nunan, 1987) or problem set forth intrinsically necessitates a certain mode of language (spoken or written) at any given point in the drama.
(3) Drama has the potential of activating the affective side of the curriculum as well as content areas from across the curriculum by involving the student emotionally and cognitively in the learning process.

Discussion

The Nature of Classroom Language

Observers of immersion classrooms are reluctant to admit that a classroom dialect or pidgin characterizes the language of immersion graduates. Students are very proficient yet their language lacks authenticity (Hammerly, 1987; Lyster, 1987). The nature of traditional tasks in the classroom, be it an L1 or L2 classroom, precludes the use of extended discourse found in the outside world (Green & Harker, 1988). In drama, the language tends to be more authentic and native-like. Drama entails using language in meaningful, real-life situations where the focus is on problem-solving and resolution of a purposeful task (Nunan, 1989). The teacher, who generally uses didactic language to conduct her class, now must switch to more of a dialectic format. She is also the sharer of knowledge, not the purveyor of knowledge and her questions are meant to stimulate thinking and reflection. These questions are quite different from the display questions to which she already knows the answers that typify much of her school day.

The children's language during drama is also quite different than that of a traditional classroom activity. There is a need to extend, create, and construct beyond the discrete-point vocabulary exercise or mundane comprehension question. There is a need to make oneself understood and to make meanings of others' utterances. Therefore, there is greater testing of language structures and searching for new lexicon to meet the needs of the current situation. As stated many times throughout this chapter, drama also extends the range of language functions and requires variation of register and stylistics in each new situation.

The teacher-in-role provides words for students as required. She negotiates meaning with students from within the drama and clarifies utterances which impede comprehension. Therefore, unlike some of the other conceptions of dramatic activities shared above, there is prompt feedback to a felt need which leads to immediate incorporation of the correct element into the story.

The excerpt which follow illustrates the points mentioned above. In this drama, based loosely on Max from *Where the Wild Things Are*, Max's mother (the teacher) and a policeman (one of the first grade students) are conversing on the phone:

S: La mamá de Max. La mamá de Max. Hello, Hello. Max está en un danger
    zone. (translation follows)
T: Y ¿Por qué? ¿Qué le pasó?
S: Le...Se...Ahora no puede leer. (Sign was in English, not Spanish.)
T: ¿No puede leer?
S: Sí. Y se va a una cave. Con los osos.
T: ¿A una cueva? ¿Y los osos se lo van a comer? Le dió, le dió. ¿Le hizo así?
    (makes slapping gesture) Pero, Max está vivo o está meurto?
S: Está...¿cómo se dice 'hurt?'
T: Oh. ¿Está hurido?
S: Sí, está mucho adido.
T: ¿Y por qué tú no lo sacas de la cueva, policía?
S: Porque mira la mapa. Porque tiene que ...
T: ¿Cómo qué no puedes hacer nada? Mi hijo está en la cueva con los osos
    y tú estás aquí. ¿Por qué tú no tienes los policías en esa cueva ahora
    mismo? ¡Andale! Ve a poner los policías y tráeme a Max.
S: Sí. Adiós.
T: Adiós.
(S: Max's mom. Max's mom. Hello, Hello. Max is in a danger zone. T: Why?
What happened? S: He can't read now. (Sign was in English and Max
only reads Spanish.) T: He can't read? S: Right. And he went into a cave.
With bears. T: In a cave? And the bears are going to eat him? And
they're slapping him around? But...is Max dead or alive? S: He's... how
do you say 'hurt?' T: Oh. He's hurt. S: Yes, he's hurt (intended) a lot. T:
Why aren't the police getting him out of the cave? S: Because they're
looking at a map. They need to... T: How can you do nothing? My son
is in a cave with bears and you're here. Why don't you have the police

in the cave right now? Get going. Call in the police and bring me to Max. S: Yes (Ma'am) goodbye. T: Goodbye.)

Students' written language undergoes many of the same modifications as in the spoken mode. If writing as a reporter about a robber at McDonald's, the language will be expository and factual in nature. The same information written from the point of view of the robber in prison to his sickly mother is likely to be more expressive and will demand a different style than in the case of the newsperson. Writing serves as a medium for clarifying emerging understanding of the situation or to preserve the moment for future reflection and recollection.

Since drama entails the creation of a story by all participants, there will obviously be more occasion for individual practice and expression than in a teacher-fronted exercise. Quite often, small groups are formed to work on a specific aspect of the problem. Their work is then incorporated into the story for all to see and hear. In this sense, there is a slight resemblance to the rehearsal-performance sequence suggested by Di Pietro (1987). In drama, however, both stages are conducted in the target language.

Below is an overview of one of the dramas conducted in this project. It is striking how often the type of language required changes and how different this language is from that of traditional school-related tasks.

The lesson began with Brett reading a story about a community to the first graders. From there he explained that a dog had been lost somewhere in the community and that we needed to come up with a plan to find her. Before entering the drama, it was decided that the dog would be found alive. The teacher assumed the role of a Spanish- speaking dog owner and the students asked questions of her to elicit a description of the dog and where it had last been seen: Brett: Do we need to ask her anything else? En español.

S1: ¿Cuántos años los perritos tienen?
T: Son...acaban de nacer. Tienen solamente dos o tres días.
S2: ¿Tú no sabes adónde está la perra? ¿Cuántos años tiene la perra?
T: No. La perra tiene como cuatro años.
S2: ¿Es grande?
T: Sí, es grande.
S2: Vamos a ver si nosotros la podemos encontrar.
T: Quizás la puedan encontrar. ¡Espero!
S3: ¿Los perritos tienen un papá?
T: Sí, pero el papá no está con los perritos.
S4: ¿Le gustan jugar?
T: No, no mucho porque están muy pequeños todavía. Acaban de nacer.
S3: ¿Qué color es?

T: La perra es café. Café con las patitas blancas. (discussion to clarify that dog got lost. did not run away.)
S5: ¿Cómo se dice 'got lost?'
T: Se perdió.
S5: ¿Dónde está el perro cuando se perdió?
S2: La perra.
T: Yo estaba caminando cerca de la tienda de zapatos...
(S1: How old are the puppies? T: They were just born. They're only two or three days old. S2: You don't know where the mother dog is? How old is the dog? T: No. The dog is around four years old. S2: Is it big? T: Yes, it's big. S2: Let's see if we can find her. T: Maybe you can find her. I hope so! S3: Do the puppies have a dad? T: Yes, but the dad isn't with the puppies. S4: Do they (the puppies) like to play? T: No, not much cause they're still very little. They were just born. S3: What color is the dog? T: The dog's light brown. Light brown with white paws. S5: How do you say 'got lost?' T: Se perdió. S5: Where is (was) the dog when it got lost? S2: The dog (f). T: I was walking near the shoe store...)

A large map of a community was hanging on the wall, and the children worked in groups of two to search for clues and speculate on the dog's whereabouts. Some drew footprints and others reported back that they had had conversations with proprietors of establishments in the community. At various points in the drama, the students contacted the dog owner to report on their findings. The distraught owner needed consoling and reassurance that her beloved pet would soon be found. Finally one child 'spotted' the dog under some bushes. A plan was formulated with Brett to rescue her and subsequently acted out by the participants. The elated owner thanked the children and embraced her dog. Just as everyone thought the trouble was over, Brett assumed the role of a dog owner who insisted that the dog was actually his lost dog. The students and the Spanish-speaking owner devised some 'tests' to see if the dog recognized its true owner. Having passed the tests, the dog and owner went merrily on their way with Brett apologizing for his mistake.

Complementing the whole language philosophy in language arts

Having examined the nature of teacher talk and student discourse, our attention turns to the second observation concerning drama in the immersion classroom. It is important to reiterate that language is a tool for discerning meaning and that one mode of language flows naturally to the next. Within the drama, when it is reasonable to write, students write. When more information is required, students consult books or brainstorm with each other. The focus, as in content-based instruction, is on 'something else' besides the language—in this case, the problem set in the drama. Paradoxically perhaps, it is when the focus is off language that children's linguistic systems seem to thrive and expand to meet their needs of expressing meanings.

Content from across the curriculum can easily be integrated into a drama. For example, in the McDonald's robbery, the cashiers needed to make change thus drawing on their knowledge of simple addition and subtraction from the first grade curriculum.

Altwerger, Edelsky & Flores (1987) remind us that the cuing systems of language (phonology, orthography, morphology, syntax, semantics, and pragmatics) are always simultaneously present and interacting in any situation requiring language. As second/foreign language educators, we are often reluctant to discard our activities that isolate one of these linguistic systems at a time. All too often, students are told that 'it is now time for a listening exercise' or that now, 'we will fill in the sentence with the correct form of the verb'. In drama, as in whole language, these cuing systems function jointly to facilitate meaning-making in a purposeful activity. Unlike the activities mentioned above, drama provides a cadre for *using* language, not practicing the use of language. An example from the work at Greystone Spanish immersion school should help clarify this distinction.

The president of Mexico was the target of an assassination attempt. Our job, as secret agents, was to gain entry into the country through customs without arousing the suspicion of the guards. We were to act like ordinary tourists or businessmen. Students broke into groups of four and wrote questions about why they were coming to Mexico, what was in their suitcase, or if they had any family members in Mexico. They were to anticipate any difficult questions the border guards might ask. During this exercise, the students were using question forms in an authentic context with a specific goal in mind. If they could not formulate and respond to these questions, they would be denied access to the country by their teacher, in role as the border guard. Dramatic tension aroused a desire within the students to extend their linguistic repertoires in order to succeed in their mission. This is a far cry from lessons on inversion or exercises that supply the answers to which students must formulate the appropriate questions.

Primary children are quite capable of accepting some fairly outlandish possibilities when working in drama. For example, in upgrading an existing zoo in Mexico, the first grade children found it quite reasonable that the animals could talk. Drama extended the idea of whole language into the world of imagination. From the science curriculum, they activated their knowledge of animal habitats and diets. In role as animals, the children pleaded for more space, more food, and more water. When they assumed the role of zoo planners, they incorporated the ideas of the animals into their plans and sketches. In the following segment, one of the children is showing his drawing of the new, improved lion cage. Other students are asking him questions:

S1: ¿Por qué es la jaula muy grande y él (pointing to lion) pequeño?

Zp (zoo planner): Porque la jaula de los leones son grande para que no se salgan.

S1: (laughing) Este león es pequeña.

T: ¿El león es pequeño, _____?

Zp: Sí.

T: Pero los leones necesitan jaulas grandes, ¿verdad? Dile a _____(S1) porque necesitan jaulas grandes.

Zp: Porque ellos se pueden salir y ellos, um, en el zoológico...si lo um,...pueden cojer y lo pueden volver a meter en la jaula.

S2: ¿El león es adentro de el jaula? ...

(S1: Why is the cage so big and the lion so small? Zp: Because lion cages are big so they won't get out. S1: This lion is small. T: Is the lion small _____, Zp: Yes. T: But lions need big cages, right? Tell _____why they need big cages. Zp: Because they could get out, um, in the zoo, so, you could catch them and return them to the cage. S2: Is the lion inside the cage? (Pointing to picture) ...

Experiencing the feelings of the pent up animals first-hand lead to more empathetic treatment in the planning of the improved zoo. This example leads us quite nicely into the last area under discussion.

The Affective Side of the Curriculum

In drama, there is obvious learning potential in terms of skills and objective knowledge. But the deepest kind of change that can take place is at the level of subjective meaning...Drama in education is primarily concerned with change in appraisal, on affective cognitive development (Bolton, 1979).

If one were to look at a school's curriculum guide, there would surely be two major types of goals or objectives present. The first would be the familiar behavioral objective: 'Given a list of ten animals, students will be able to classify them as vertebrates or non- vertebrates with 80% accuracy'. The second type would read something like this: 'Students will explore and appreciate the ideals and traditions of other individuals and cultures'.

The first type of objective is best met by way of traditional classroom activities such as describing the characteristics of animals or separating pictures of animals into the two classes. However, without evoking the realm of feelings and human emotion, how could a true appreciation for other cultures possibly be derived by simple description and comparison? As children age, more and more of the information they encounter in the classroom benefits their objective world knowledge. Emotional and social growth occur only in terms of experiences the child has met in life.

Through drama, the teacher is able to create situations which require children to grow socially and emotionally as well as academically. In drama, there are actually two complementary plays going on simultaneously. The students' play has a 'what's going to happen next' orientation while the teacher's is more concerned with educational goals. Bolton has identified four features that must be present to ensure learning on the affective cognitive level: (1) sharing: group members collectively identify with a selected form of make believe, (2) congruency: feelings must match the objective meaning, (3) ascendancy of the collective over the personal level of subjectivity, and (4) a feeling of quality: i.e. if someone dies, genuine feelings of sadness prompted by the drama occur.

During a drama based on the story *Dónde Viven Los Monstruos* (Where The Wild Things Are), Brett explained that Max was missing and that his mother was quite upset at his disappearance. The children, through Brett's subtle questions and suggestions, decided to play consoling friends of the mother or policemen intent on finding Max. As the drama unfolded, the policemen located a hurt Max in a bear cave. It was then decided that some children would play ambulance drivers, doctors, and nurses while others continued to console the mother. After a lengthy hospital stay, Max returned home and was regaled with a party by his relieved friends and family.

Brett exercised the option of adjusting the field (situation or context), tenor (relationship among the roles), or mode (spoken or written) of this drama to promote whole class brainstorming, small group work, or approaching the task 'as experts' (policemen or medical personnel). Each manipulation of the situation changed the manner in which the drama participants needed to interact with each other. Looking at a few of these social interactions, we have: the distraught mother and her well-meaning friends, the policemen tempering their professional expertise with empathetic concern for the mother, and doctors and nurses agonizing over the correct treatment to save a life. The children's sociolinguistic competence was surely put to the test in order to deal successfully with each type of interaction. The excerpt that follows is part of the conversation between the teacher in role as Max's mother and one of her first graders in role as a doctor. Notice how the student must rely on the teacher's help to incorporate new vocabulary to express his thoughts. The written transcription alone, devoid of all gestures and intonation, necessitates that you, the reader, call upon your own world knowledge to breathe life into this exchange.

S: Sra. S.....Se um, um, tiene.. ¿Cómo se dice 'ribs?'
T: ¿Las costillas?
S: Tiene, tiene.. ¿Cómo se dice un 'little string?'
T: Un hilito.
S: Un hilito. ¿Cómo se dice 'hold?'
T: Aguantándola.
S: Un hilito aguantando la costilla.
T: ¿La costilla?
S: Sí.
T: Y eso, ¿por qué?
S: ¿Cómo se dice 'string?'
T: Hilo.
S: Cuando la hilo se um...
S2: Corto.
T: ¿Todas las costillas se van a caer? ¿Qué vas a hacer tú? ¿Tú eres el médico?
S: Sí. ¿Cómo se dice 'We are trying our best?'
T: ¿Y qué vas a hacer para que Max se ponga bien?
(S: Mrs. S...How do you say 'ribs?' T: costillas. S: He has, he has, how do you say 'a little string?' T: 'un hilito'. S: A little string. How do you say 'hold?' T: aquantándola. S: A little string is holding the rib. T: the rib? S: Yes. T: And why is that? S: How do you say 'string?' T: Hilo. S: When the string...S2: breaks... T: All the ribs are going to fall? What are you going to do? Are you the doctor? S: Yes. How do you say 'We're trying our best?' T: And what are you going to do so Max will get better?)

In a traditional classroom with the teacher up front, the usual sequence of interaction goes something like this: the teacher initiates the exchange, the students respond, and the teacher makes some sort of evaluation (IRE interaction). As evidenced above, the variety of social interactions is potentially increased through drama. Socially appropriate behaviors and awareness are also activated. When a child is missing, we search for him. When he is found hurt, we take him to the hospital. When he has recuperated, we have a celebration.

A group representation or symbolization emerges out of a drama such as the Max drama. This is the affective cognitive knowledge Bolton refers to which leads to greater understanding of what it is to be a human being with feelings and decisions to make. Certainly the children's factual knowledge of what a policeman does and how hospital personnel rely on X-rays and monitors aided in the resolution of the crisis. Yet instead of simply describing or listing what one does in the case of an emergency, these students have lived through this experience. They have a common foundation to draw upon in their future resolution of life's problems. It would not be surprising to hear one of them say: 'Hey, remember when Max was missing and we called the police in? Why don't we do the same thing now to help us find the kid who didn't come back from recess?'

Conclusion

The concept of ownership is quite prevalent in research on learning. Others have discussed promoting learner autonomy through awareness of learning strategies (see O'Malley, Holec & Wenden in Wenden & Rubin 1987). The Vygotskyan perspective holds that a learner must pass through three phases to arrive at true understanding: object regulation (basic skills), other regulation (what the teacher wants me to learn), and self regulation or true internalization of the content.

Much of the aforementioned discussion on drama has alluded to this very same idea. Drama provides an arena where participants must make decisions collaboratively to complete a mission. They bring to the task their knowledge and experience of the world to which the teacher adds new knowledge in the form of resource materials from across the curriculum provided strategically along the way. An intrinsic need motivates students to research, write, discuss, plan, read, listen and resolve the problem. The direction the drama assumes is left to the discretion of the group based upon the reasonableness of the idea.

These elements lead naturally to ownership on the part of the learner. Passive acceptance of teacher-mandated activities is foreign in a drama activity. Rather, it is the group's representation of the situation that necessitates certain logical steps (activities) to complete the task.

Drama in an immersion setting not only provides ownership of the curricular content but of the linguistic content as well. Through use, in meaningful contexts, students are able to hypothesize, test, and modify their language to meet the demands of the situation. Sociolinguistic competence is called upon as well as grammatical and strategic competence. Attempts at meaning-making are motivated from within rather than from without as in so many foreign/second language classroom activities.

Further Research

Incorporating drama in an immersion setting was quite successful in terms of content (both social and subject matter) and target language development. Questions remain concerning the generalizability of this technique to other foreign/second language settings.

(1) Would students in a core program at the junior high or senior high school level where the majority of us teach foreign languages possess the linguistic proficiency to work in drama?

(2) Would university students accustomed to more of a discrete-point, grammatical approach accept this type of activity?

(3) Would adult second language learners be able to shed their inhibitions and be willing to call upon their imaginations in problem- solving tasks?

These are but a few of the options open to researchers interested in studying drama in the foreign/second language classroom. The variables of age, proficiency level, setting, teaching styles, learning styles, etc. would also have to be considered to provide us with a more complete picture of the effectiveness of drama in the second language classroom.

4 Whole Language and Literature in a French Immersion Elementary School

JANET HICKMAN

Introduction

From the outset, one of the goals of the French immersion project at Ecole Glenwood was to encourage and to study the implementation of whole language teaching in that environment, with particular attention to the use of culturally authentic children's literature. As a part of the research team I was challenged to look at immersion teaching from the perspective of an elementary school educator. I was encouraged to study immersion *not* as a person interested in second language acquisition or in the learning of French in particular, but rather as one interested in children who learn and use language to explore the world.

I was a firsthand observer of these efforts during the second year of the project (the school's third year of operation) and also, via videotapes, of the project's first year. As a specialist in children's literature, I consulted with teachers on possible choices as well as on possible uses of children's books in their classrooms. I talked with teachers, with the library aide, with the principal, and an occasional parent.

I found that, in spite of the inherently close relationship of whole language teaching, literature, and language learning, and in spite of good intentions all around, the recommended approaches appeared difficult for teachers to implement—sometimes verging on the unworkable. I want to suggest here that in retrospect, these difficulties were not too surprising. Most of them are common to other schools and teachers in the process of working toward whole language teaching. Some of the difficulties, however, seem tied to the nature of the immersion enterprise itself.

Whole Language and Authentic Text

Whole language is not an easy term to define. It refers to a philosophy or a cluster of theories that underlies teaching rather than to a specific set of methods or a particular package of materials. In part, the antecedents of whole language are in Progressive education and in the British infant schools of recent decades, where it has been unlabeled, as Moira McKenzie says, except as 'good teaching' (Stephens *et al.*, 1990). While these theories and the methods that embody them have enjoyed high level sanction and dissemination in Britain, Canada, New Zealand, and Australia for some time, the movement toward whole language in the United States owes more to the grass-roots enthusiasm of individual teachers than to the leadership of influential academics and teacher training institutions. Among practitioners, interpretations of whole language may vary considerably.

Among scholars, however, proponents of whole language generally seem to agree on some basic features. One feature is that teachers should take full advantage of the kinship between oral language learning and literacy learning. Cambourne (1984) outlined seven conditions under which children learn to talk (immersion, demonstration, expectation, responsibility, approximation, employment, feedback) and challenged teachers to recreate those conditions in their efforts to help children deal with the written medium. Halliday (1975) emphasized meaning and function in children's development of oral language, and his work is often cited as a base for emphasizing functional uses of print as children develop literacy skills. Goodman's (1986) book *What's Whole in Whole Language?* which has been so widely read by practitioners that it assumes definitive proportions, underscores the value of learning both oral and written language in the context of use so that literacy tasks have a natural function. He emphasizes the importance of whole texts and connected discourse, books written by 'real writers who have something to say' (p. 28) rather than 'non-texts' that result from the over-controlled vocabulary, choppy sentences, and unpredictable plots of many written-to-order materials.

This use of authentic texts is one of the hallmarks of a whole language classroom, where children's literature becomes, in large part, the content of the reading program. Students' skills in reading and in interpreting literature develop as they listen to, read, write about, talk about, and in many other ways respond to stories. There is a growing body of research that demonstrates growth in vocabulary (Bridge, Winograd & Haley, 1983; Cohen, 1968; Elley, 1989) and in comprehension (Reutzel & Fawson, 1989; Roser, Hoffman, & Farest, 1990; Wollman-Bonilla, 1989) associated with such methods. Encouragement for the use of children's books also comes from studies indicating that classrooms which provide many experiences with literature nurture voluntary reading (Morrow & Weinstein, 1986) and produce high levels of literary response (Hickman, 1981; Lehr, 1988; McClure, Harrison & Reed, 1990).

With its focus on speaking, reading, and writing for personal and functional purposes and with the vast array of published works of children's literature from which it may draw, whole language teaching has the advantage of great flexibility. Being based on principles rather than specific materials, methods can be adapted to various teaching situations as well as to individual children. In practice, whole language classrooms may look quite different from one another, although they tend to share certain recognizable features. For instance, Ridley's (1990) description of whole language in an ESL classroom touches on individual children writing in response to their own experiences and to stories they have heard, children talking together and sharing purposeful work in pairs and small groups, children reading on their own and reading together, and children exploring a theme through selected literature. Similar activities in countless variation have been reported in elementary and middle school classrooms in many settings (Atwell, 1987; Avery, 1987; Newkirk, 1989; Van Dongen, 1987).

With this sort of adaptability and with such strong ties to oral language learning, it seems that whole language should be a natural approach for immersion schooling. Moreover, the ready appeal of children's literature and its demonstrated effectiveness for literacy learning makes this aspect of such a program especially desirable. What happens, then, when immersion teachers are encouraged to implement whole language and draw on children's literature as authentic texts?

Looking at immersion classrooms

In order to see what holistic methods are used to nurture literacy at a French immersion school, a visitor might focus not on the children's fluency in French (surely an important question, though a different one) but on evidence of ongoing work in the classroom, how it operates, and what purposes are served. Is what happens here similar in basic features or in principle to what happens in well-established English whole language programs? To clarify the question we might narrow our range of concerns to three general principles demonstrated over and over again in descriptions of successful whole language classrooms:

(1) children's opportunities to produce language—to speak, write, and read in a variety of personal-social contexts;

(2) children's engagement in activities that call for meaningful, purposeful uses of oral and written language rather than practice for its own sake;
(3) children's access to a variety of appropriate books and experiences with literature.

With these principles in mind, we can consider the following vignettes from Glenwood immersion classrooms.

Fifth grade

Mme P. conducts morning content lessons entirely in French. On this day children are seated in two rows of desks on opposite sides of the classroom, facing each other across a wide aisle. Having gone over the day's schedule and assignments written on the chalkboard, the teacher asks questions about yesterday's weather and today's weather, coaxing short answers from volunteers. Her focus settles on temperature and the number vocabulary needed to express it. At that point the classroom intercom crackles on, and a younger child's voice announces the day's school news, in French. There is an undercurrent of murmuring at the end, with fifth graders apparently more interested in the other student's delivery than in the content of the announcements.

Mme P. moves on into the math lesson she has planned to help children learn and use the vocabulary of numbers and dates. She reads aloud a computational problem from the board, asking volunteers to give the answer. After a brief period in which all children work silently on a paper and pencil problem, Mme P. directs their attention to another section of the chalkboard, where significant dates are written. She calls on individual children to read specified dates aloud to the class. Then Mme passes out paper, explaining how students are to head it, and begins a dictation activity for which she reads dates that children are to transcribe into numerical form (the first is *le quatre juillet, mille sept cent soixante six* [July 4, 1766]). Although she does not call for repetition, some children can be heard echoing her words softly as they begin to write.

After an extended interruption for the class's vocal music period, the number work continues. The teacher names other dates, and children attempt to transpose and write them, first at their seats, then at the chalkboard. Answers to a previous assignment are shared at the end of the time, with eager volunteers hurrying to the board to display their solutions. In fact, one of the notable things about this observation time is the enthusiasm and level of engagement shown by most of the children, who respond as if they are playing a game, as if each right answer or even each good try might be a point won.

First grade

Mme L'.s first grade class is conducted entirely in French, all day, every day. When children have questions or comments in English, as they frequently do, she asks for French. Whether or not an attempt is forthcoming, her response is in French. On this winter morning they are seated in rows facing the chalkboard beginning to write in their journals two sentences they have already read together from large teacher-made charts. One gives the date: *Aujourd'hui c'est mardi le 6 février, 1990* [Today is Tuesday, February 6, 1990]. The other calls for a personal response to a brief, already familiar rhyme: *Voici ce qui me rend content(e) et heureux(se)* [Here is what makes me content and happy]. Mme L. gives repeated demonstrations of using the proper endings as determined by the gender of the writer. She questions individual children about which endings they will use and reminds them they are to draw a picture of something that makes them happy to accompany this sentence.

As the class sets to work (not all children seem equally engaged in this activity), Mme assembles a small group on the rug in the reading area. They read in unison from small booklets. It is a familiar text, and most members of the group are able to continue as the teacher softens her voice and drops out of the lead from time to time. When this reading is complete, Mme chooses some members of the group to mime the action of the story as she reads the text. Non-participants squirm; she changes the cast of characters and repeats the activity so all group members have a chance to take part.

In the next order of business, Mme L. reads to the group from another booklet, again from a text that is greeted like an old friend. Although the only illustration is on the cover, the children are attentive as Mme reads couplets about animals doing nonsensical things. One child volunteers the comment that it rhymes. Mme agrees and repeats a portion of the text as a chant, accenting the rhythm and rhyme. 'You make it sound like a song!' says another child. Later, when rewards of hard candy are meted out for positive behavior, Mme begins a chant in the same form, featuring the word *bonbon* [candy]. She invites the children to furnish rhyming words, and with her help they supply *ballon, bon, mouton*, and *maison*, all of which she writes on the board, pointing out the common endings.

Fourth grade

During the second year of the project, Mme P. teaches fourth grade. In keeping with school policy she offers a block of reading/language arts instruction in English. Mid year, she expresses interest in finding a children's novel, preferably historical fiction, that she can read aloud to the class and use as a basis for writing and reading as well as other activities. She settles on *Sarah, Plain and Tall* by Patricia MacLachlan (1985), the story of a pioneer family made whole when a mail-order bride from Maine agrees to stay on the prairie with a farmer and his two lonely children. By spring Mme has obtained multiple copies of the book plus resource materials and has laid some plans. She intends to include some reinforcement work in French as the study progresses.

The read-aloud sessions, viewing of a filmstrip version, and a few writing activities (including composing a mock newspaper advertisement for a spouse) are finished in early May. On this observation afternoon the emphasis is on wildflowers, that having been an interest of the book's title character. Activity suggestions are listed on the board, including the possibility of making up a song about a flower, as one of the characters had done in the book. After children share results of the previous day's book-related activity, which was compiling a list of many ways of saying 'yes' in English and other languages, Mme P. announces that the class will make 'a flower book'. She introduces several informational books on flowers and plants. These are to be left on a work table for children to look through.

Then Mme P. tells the group that since there are so many comparisons in the novel between Maine and the prairie, she has chosen a picture book that takes place in Maine to read aloud to them. The book is *Miss Rumphius* by Barbara Cooney (1982); some children are familiar with it. 'Oh, it's good!' one says. 'It's where she spreads flowers all over'. As the teacher reads, children have a few spontaneous questions. Most of the comments are from Mme P. who points out similarities and differences between settings and characters in the two books: 'Sarah brought a lot of shells with her, too', 'You see the difference between this and the prairie, I'm sure'.

When Miss Rumphius sows the seeds of lupines, Mme P. asks if that reminds the class of anything. One answer is immediate—'Johnny Apple-seed'. The teacher smiles, and pauses at the last few lines of text, where it becomes clear that Miss Rumphius had indeed made the world more beautiful, as she was advised to do. The children chime in with several suggestions for ways they could contribute to this effort. 'We could make the world more beautiful if people would stop taking marijuana and crack', one boy says.

Later, as children begin to work at their seats on constructing definitions for 'interesting words' they had previously identified from the book, Mme tells the class she has located a French translation of the story, titled *Sarah, la Pas Belle*. There is some muttering about what that term means. One girl says, aloud, 'But she *was* pretty, in her own way'. Mme smiles. 'Exactly', she says.

Looking for whole language

What we get from quick glimpses such as these of Glenwood immersion classrooms is a picture of teachers working very hard to provide a focus on language across the curriculum and to keep children involved and interested. The staff in general expressed high regard for whole language principles and great interest in working with literature. Using the preceding vignettes as touchpoints, we can consider here the degree to which those ideas and intentions appeared actually to govern instruction. The results are mixed.

Do children have opportunities to use language in a variety of personal-social contexts? In the first two examples class was conducted in French. In spite of efforts to get children to speak and write in French, it was the teacher who actually produced most of the language, both oral and written. When children spoke, it was most often to the teacher, with the whole class as audience. Unison reading provided some variation. Children did talk to each other occasionally, in English, but this was an unsanctioned activity.

In the last example, where class was conducted in English, children did volunteer and respond more readily. They had been invited to write in various forms, and their spontaneous comments as well as direct answers were welcomed during the reading and brief discussion of *Miss Rumphius*. Children could be expected to be more productive with their native language, of course, but it is unclear how the use of literature may have influenced this productivity. Teachers of English at all levels often report that well-chosen books are good for generating discussion and motivating writing. In any event, the prevalence of whole group activities and whole group as audience for sharing individual efforts at a common assignment did limit the range of contexts in which children used language.

Are children engaged in functional, personally meaningful uses of language? In these examples it is apparent that the sanctioned purposes for using language were set by the teacher to meet curricular goals. (Even the child on the intercom reading school announcements, a functional task, was dealing with someone else's news.) Most children adopted official purposes cheerfully enough and attempted to meet expectations. In both languages, the truly functional conversations in which children participated had to do with class procedures and assignments, getting directions, and negotiating the tasks and relationships that constitute classroom culture.

It would be unfortunate to assume that children had no opportunities to establish their own goals or to pursue discussion, reading, and writing to satisfy a personal or group need. Classroom and bulletin board displays throughout the school showed that letters were sometimes written for real communicative purposes, original ideas turned into stories for other students to read, community support projects begun and followed through. What must be noted, however, is that such activities seemed to be 'add-ons'. In whole language teaching one would expect them to be everyday occurrences, the very foundation of the language program.

Do children have adequate access to books and a variety of experiences with literature? The answer to this question seems to be a qualified yes. Mme. L. shared rhymes and stories in French with her first graders from booklets made for instruction. In English language/whole language classrooms, similar materials such as the Story Box Books might be in use. However, these would usually be supported by the presence of and by ready reference to a generous collection of well-illustrated picture books.

Mme P'.s study of one book in English with her fifth graders certainly falls within the common bounds of practice by teachers who identify themselves as using literature-based instruction. Whether or not it fully implemented the principles of whole language, the day's activity did put children in touch with several books in different genres within a framework of common threads of meaning. What is probably most notable about this literature study, however, is that it was not routine. Middle grade students in well established whole language programs have regular, built-in opportunities to revisit and consider literature through writing, discussion, and other activities.

Looking at the school as a whole, there were of course other indicators of children's access to literature, from bulletin boards that reflected favorite stories to books waiting on student desktops to be read. Although classroom book collections were generally small, considerable effort had been made to assemble a school library collection in two languages. Classrooms were scheduled for double library times each week, so that the regular library aide could read aloud or introduce books in English while the classroom teacher could do the same for books in French. Lively library programs are characteristic of whole language schools in general. In most such schools, however, reading aloud is seen as such an important activity by teachers that more emphasis is placed on read-aloud in the classroom than in the library.

Issues and Problems

At Glenwood, then, there are teachers who have been encouraged to adopt whole language teaching in an immersion setting. They express high regard for those ideas and for the use of children's literature. Yet observations at Glenwood did not show teachers or children engaged in the same range of activities, nor with the same emphases, as those commonly found in established whole language classrooms (Hickman, 1983; Mills & Clyde, 1990). In part, this seems to be due to the same difficulties experienced by English language teachers across the United States who have opted for or been directed to change from familiar modes of teaching to whole language.

The first of these issues concerns teacher training and long term support. Without specific training in the theories of learning and language that undergird this approach, and without a period of mentorship or other support during which these ideas can be internalized, all but the most remarkably intuitive teachers experience a struggle. Whole language implies, among other things, a shift of control away from the teacher toward the student that requires the rethinking of seemingly simple classroom routines as well as traditional instructional procedures. A teacher's earlier training may make this stance difficult for him or her to adopt, a problem generic to teacher change. By their own reckoning most whole language teachers need several years to develop the requisite skills and confidence in using them.

A second issue faced by Glenwood teachers but not unique to them or to immersion schooling is that of real or perceived pressures, such as time constraints, administrative requirements and expectations, and parent concerns. It can be argued that immersion intensifies all these pressures, with or without the effort toward whole language teaching. It can also be argued that certain types of expectations create more of a barrier to whole language than do others. For reading instruction in English at Glenwood, which began officially at grade two, teachers were expected to work with the school system's basal reader program, at least to the point of 'covering' that material. Goodman (1986) considers whole language by definition antithetical to basal reader instruction; certainly there are critical differences between the two sets of underlying principles. For immersion teachers to successfully implement whole language in their teaching of French and the procedures of basal reading instruction in English would require a firm command of both approaches and enormous concentration in keeping the two separate. Thus the pressure of making time to instruct in two languages would be made more stressful by dealing with the dissonance in methods.

Some of the difficulties in implementing a whole language/literature based approach at Glenwood, however, are a direct result of its being a French immersion school in the American Midwest. One of these is a lack of authentic texts, or 'real' books for children in French. These materials are crucial for a program that involves wide reading and individual choice. Unlike English language classrooms where complaints may be heard because there are not sufficient funds to purchase a full range of books, for French classrooms there may not be enough material available for purchase to satisfy a full range of needs.

Primary teachers pointed out that Glenwood's considerable library collection of picture books in French contained few titles that were appropriate for reading aloud to children with minimal command of the language or that could support children's own beginning efforts at reading and writing. Such books would have simple story lines, preferably with repetitive patterns occurring naturally in the text, and illustrations that clearly support meaning. Many of the books popular with children in French-speaking countries do not fit those criteria, as one teacher demonstrated by pulling European favorites off the library shelves to show minimal or impressionistic illustrations and large amounts of text. Many books that do fit the criteria are available in English, however. Some editions in translation were available in the Glenwood library. Also teachers reported that for desired books published only in English, they frequently translated as they read or even wrote out a French text on adhesive paper and used it to cover the English words, creating their own print translation.

Even these measures, apparently, do not serve for all potentially good titles. One book in English with which teachers of beginning readers have consistent success is *The Chick and the Duckling* by Mirra Ginsburg (1972). This text is already a translation, from the Russian of V. Suteyev, but ironically, teachers reported that their attempts to tell the story in French did not capture its crisp language patterns. Moreover, the vocabulary when translated requires children to deal with sounds particularly difficult for beginners. First grade teacher Mme T. identified Bill Martin Jr'.s (1983) *Brown Bear, Brown Bear, What Do You See?* as a book that does work well in translation. The search for good titles continues.

For older students with more proficiency but a still limited command of French, the availability of authentic children's books in that language is even more problematic. Although some picture books do speak to the natural interests of nine and ten year olds, most do not. On the other end of the scale, longer novels require more fluency in French than most of the Glenwood students had yet acquired. Books at a transitional level of difficulty are hard to find in English and much less available in French.

Since the older children's work also included reading and language arts in English, one might expect that they would have had richer contacts with literature in that context. However, teachers who as children themselves did not speak English are not likely to know the repertoire of children's books in English as a native speaker would. Such teachers will have limitations in the range of children's literature they know well enough to recommend to young readers. Nonnative speakers of English may also be more reluctant to present books in English. At least one Glenwood teacher expressed discomfort with the prospect of reading long books aloud; it would take much practice, she said, to perfect the intonation and pacing.

While the lack of certain types of children's books in French and the limits of teachers' acquaintance with children's books in English were conditions that worked against a reliance on authentic texts in this immersion setting, both those conditions are subject to improvement. Another issue, however, seemed to pose a far greater challenge to the full implementation of whole language teaching at Glenwood, as it must in other, similar settings. Teachers at Glenwood, and the primary teachers in particular, carry the burden of being chief supplier and sole arbiter of the spoken language that children are to learn. This is a marked contrast to Cambourne's (1984) discussion of 'immersion' as a condition of children's natural language learning and a model for whole language teaching:

> From the moment they are born, meaningful spoken language washes over and surrounds children. They are *immersed* in a 'language flood' and, for most of their waking time, proficient users of the language-culture that they happen to have been born into literally bathe them in the sounds, meanings, cadences and rhythms of the language that they have to learn (p. 6).

For all practical purposes the only 'proficient user' talking regularly to a child at Glenwood was his or her own classroom teacher.

One first grade teacher reported that in her previous positions in France and in Quebec, where 'kids had the same language...you don't have to act out, you talk less. Here we have to repeat and repeat every day'. The necessity of providing both the language and the nonverbal cues that make it meaningful puts the teacher in a particular relation to students. My own notes after visiting one of the primary classrooms at Glenwood recorded this impression: 'Style totally animated. Children need to be focused on her much of the time'. Whole language teaching, on the other hand, assumes the possibility of encouraging social interaction and the empowerment of students to use language to their own ends. These are difficult goals to achieve while children are watching the teacher for basic communication clues.

The development of literacy in whole language classrooms builds on children's competence and confidence with oral language and their familiarity with print materials. Goodman (1986) describes it this way:

> Children read familiar, meaningful wholes first, predictable materials that draw on concepts and experiences they already have: signs, cereal

boxes, T-shirts, and books. Soon they will spot familiar words and phrases in new wholes, and it won't be long before they are able to handle unfamiliar words and phrases in familiar uses anywhere—with no worries for the teacher about a sequence or hierarchy of skills (p. 43).

In whole language classrooms bent on developing literacy in the mother tongue, children are surrounded in school, at home, and in the community with 'familiar, meaningful wholes'. Even in most United States settings where English is taught as a second language, it is the dominant language; there are ample resources of environmental print in English, meaningful and whole although perhaps less immediately familiar to students. But the Glenwood children live in the Midwest, where 'signs, cereal boxes, T-shirts and books' do *not* display the language they are trying to learn. That means, again, that their attention turns to the teacher, who provides the French language for them and tries to find ways to make words and phrases familiar and meaningful. In the Midwest there are so few sources of reinforcement that occur naturally for learners of French (an occasional menu, a small scattering of native speakers as visitors or, rarely, residents) that the school and its teachers are really going it alone.

Another perspective is to consider that whole language learning is always seen as a constructivist activity, with children's risk-taking and a trial and error approach in producing language as a necessary part of the description. The acceptance of overgeneralization in grammatical forms, of invented spellings in early writing, and of meaningful approximations in reading are manifestations of this aspect of whole language. These forms are accepted because teachers are confident that children will develop facility with conventional forms by means of the feedback they get through experience with multiple sources of oral and written language. The load created for an immersion teacher in a culture that does not speak the language is immense. When the teacher is the only proficient language user within the child's world—school, home, community—it is only the teacher's response that can really help the child become more proficient. As the students themselves gain experience with print and as their classmates acquire the language and begin to respond to each other, this situation becomes less critical. Still, however, the teacher is nudged toward a role that seems, by whole language standards, to be invested with undue authority. Nor is it a small matter that this role is exhausting; the teacher must talk, use gestures, act out, repeat, respond, write, read it back, and more. The responsibility for creating a French-speaking world for immersion students in the American Midwest seemed most burdensome because it was so solitary.

Conclusions

It would be inappropriate to look at the experience of Glenwood teachers and conclude that whole language is simply too problematic an approach for an immersion school. Certainly some specific applications of whole language teaching worked well, such as the repeated readings of simple patterned stories to encourage a variety of oral and written responses and to establish a shared knowledge of printed text. In spite of difficulties in locating age-appropriate and culturally authentic children's books, teachers did find ways to incorporate literature in various subject areas. And there were many indications that teachers saw themselves as still developing their roles and their methods, still refining their procedures.

What seems to call for concern, and for closer examination, is the way in which the underpinnings of whole language shift when language learning is neither in the mother tongue nor in a language in general home and community use: the natural context for learning a language narrows to the school and classroom, the support base of proficient users shrinks dramatically, to classroom teacher and colleagues. The watchwords 'relevant' and 'functional' take on different meanings from the way in which they are used in a first language setting. In a regular whole language elementary school classroom, 'relevant' and 'functional' have immediacy attached to their respective semantic fields. Children learn and use language *in* school that empowers them when they *leave* school for the day.

In the immersion settings I observed, this 'immediacy' was not possible. Indeed children were learning and using language in school that was relevant and functional in that school setting. In some sense this learning empowers them with greater knowledge about the world around them. But, in the American Midwest, this is a distant world—a world that will perhaps never be encountered—and one which has not established the curriculum that the children are to follow. It is a world that is characterized by a different oral language base, a different sense of literacy, and a different set of social conventions and socio-political aspirations.

The concept of 'whole language' in a second language immersion setting is not built on the same set of assumptions as 'whole language' in a first language setting. 'Whole' and 'natural' in the immersion setting have been redefined. The implementation of whole language teaching in an immersion setting requires a domain-specific understanding of language immersion teaching so that whole language insights can be used to their best advantage.

5 Student–Teacher Interactions in Selected French Immersion Classrooms

ANN MASTERS SALOMONE

French immersion education began in 1965 as an attempt to produce bilingual students in Canada, where speaking French in addition to English can be a definite advantage both economically and culturally. Offering instruction in French to anglophone children was construed simply as a change in the tool for instruction. Content was to remain the same; only the vehicle for its transfer and acquisition would change.

After a quarter of a century, however, it appears that the double goals of achievement in subject matter learning and bilingualism for all students are not so simply attained. Increasingly, scholars are questioning both the product of immersion and its process. Criticisms range from claims of students' grammatical inaccuracy (e.g. Lyster, 1987) to challenges leveled at the depth of thought processing in the immersion classroom (e.g. Lapkin & Swain with Shapson, 1990). Data from this study suggest that a closer investigation of these criticisms is warranted.

The present study is a secondary analysis of data collected for other purposes (see Salomone, this volume). One strength of these data rests on the amount of time the researcher spent in observation. Five elementary French immersion teachers were observed for 15+ hours each and the kindergarten teacher for 10+ hours—a total of 85+ hours of observation. In addition, sponsorship by a US Department of Education grant (#R168F80060) provided funds for two-hour videotapes of each of these teachers. Data derived from the field notes taken during observations, and these were supported and enhanced by what had been recorded on video.

Student Grammatical Errors: The Product

If we turn our attention to the most common charges against immersion education—grammatical inaccuracy in student French—we find much support for such critiques. The immersion product (student L2) has been studied extensively for over 20 years. Overall, researchers are pleased with the fluency and language sense of immersion students. Several researchers, however, question whether the unstructured *use* of the second language is a sufficient means to the achievement of bilingualism as needed for adequate language functioning and true sensitivity to francophone cultural issues. Harley (1984) evaluated immersion students' communicative competence, including grammatical competence, discourse competence, sociolinguistic competence, and strategic competence (see Canale & Swain, 1980). She found that grade 5/6 immersion students still erred fairly consistently in terms of grammar, but that their discourse and strategic competence seemed to compensate for this lack of accurate speech. She concluded that sociolinguistic competence was also not well-developed by grade 6.

Spilka (1976) found that immersion students not only erred grammatically but also that some of their errors persisted throughout their elementary school years. Pellerin & Hammerly (1986) discovered similar errors in the students that they studied and were disheartened to note that the errors persisted until the 12th grade. Pawley (1985) evaluated both primary and late-entry immersion students, who generally ranked at the 2 or 2+ level on the Foreign Service Interview Test. She concluded that French immersion students' speaking ability is their weakest skill. Lyster (1987) asserted that French immersion students 'speak immersion'—a pidgin dialect of French—and that new methodologies are needed to eradicate the inaccuracies in both grammatical and sociolinguistic competence of immersion students.

Student errors were also recorded in the data for this study. We will group them according to the categories used by Selinker, Swain & Dumas in their study of children's interlanguage (1975): language transfer, overgeneralization of target language rules, and simplification. *Language transfer* errors occur when the learner constructs a sentence in the L2 the same way he or she would in the native language (L1). These include inserting an English word in a French sentence. Some examples from our second-graders:

'Je suis allé voir la course de voitures dans le *building* de mon papa'. [I went to see the car race in my father's *building*.]

'Je suis allé à la *race*'. [I went to the *race*.]

Using *être* when *avoir* was required occurred often at Glenwood School:

'Ma frère est 12. Ma maman est 32'. [My brother is (has) 12 (years). My mother is (has) 32 (years).]

'Je suis beaucoup de sous aussi'. [I am (have) many cents also.]

What Selinker *et al.* call the English process of stranding of prepositions was recorded in our study also: 'Quel groupe est Jim dans?' [What group is Jim in?] (not a grammatically correct construction in French).

Common to both Selinker's study and ours was the discovery that immersion students place adjectives before the noun, as in English:

'Le petit rouge poisson '... [The little red fish . . .]

'Madame, n'oubliez pas anglais bibliothèque'. [Madame, don't forget English library.]

'Un grand bleu carré'. [A big blue square.]

Not mentioned by Selinker, but noted in our study, transfer errors included the use of English verbal structures when speaking French. In the following cases, conjugated verbs were used where infinitives are required in French:

'Je peux *va* à la toilette?' [I can go to the toilet?]

'Je peux *écrit* "le garçon donne la carotte aux lapins"?' [I can write 'the boy gives the carrot to the rabbits'?]

'Tu peux *va* dans la rue . . '. [You can go in the street . . .]

We also recorded an avoidance of the French *possession + de + possessor construction*:

'La souris queue est très longue'. [The mouse tail is very long.]

Overgeneralization of L2 usage included overuse of the most familiar verb forms. In our first example, a first-person verb form is used with a third-person pronoun; in the second, a second-person plural form is used with a first-person singular pronoun; and in the third, a singular verb is used with a plural pronoun:

'Il n'ai pas des crayons'. [He have no crayons.]

'Je dansez'. [I dance.]

'Ils dit'. [They says.] (written error)

Using *avoir* as an auxiliary when *être* is required for the past tense was common:

'J'ai allé'. [I went.]

'J'ai resté au maison'. [I stayed at home.]

'J'ai tombé'. [I fell.] (2 instances)

and vice versa:

'Mlle, je suis fini'. [Miss, I am finished.]

(3 instances, at least 2 students)

Simplification strategies included overuse of infinitives when conjugated verbs were required by the context:

'Un singe vient et prendre le chapeau et mettre sur sa tête'. [A monkey comes and to take the hat and to put on his head.]

As evidence of a lack of sociolinguistic competence as well as a possible simplification error, students were sometimes overheard using the tu form to address their teachers (noted also by Harley, 1984):

'Mlle, regarde le sapin'. [Miss, look at (familiar) the evergreen tree.]

A study by Frauenfelder (1974, cited in Selinker *et al.*, 1975) found that 10 seven-and-a-half year olds marked masculine nouns correctly 93% of the time, but feminine nouns were correctly marked only 46% of the time. Although our study yielded no percentages, we found that students often simplified the L2 by using the same gender articles for all nouns. From written data, I believed that students always overused masculine articles. However, a re-analysis of the videotapes showed that at least one student used feminine noun-markers exclusively. Although students used 'sa nom,' 'un carotte,' 'un personne,' 'le bicyclette' (written), 'mon maman,' 'le neige,' 'au maison,' 'le dent,' 'un feuille,' 'un balançoire,' 'un souris grise,' and 'un grenouille,' one third-grader stated during a math lesson: 'J'ai une question. Si tu as une sept ici et une une ici . . '. [I have a question. If you have a seven here and a one here . . .]

Pronouns were also troublesome for our immersion students, who used disjunctive and object pronouns interchangeably:

'Mon cousin est venu chez me'. (instead of moi) [My cousin came to my house.]

'Madame, il frappé moi' and 'Tu skippé moi'. (instead of 'Il m'a frappé' and 'Tu m'a skippé'.) [Madam, he hit me] and [You skipped me.]

Students showed their lack of vocabulary often and mixed words up. They confused *savoir* and *connaître*, *parler* and *dire*, *tableau* and *table*, *patte* and *jambe*, *Mexico* and *Mexique*, and *hôtel* and *maison*.

How teachers correct or do not correct these errors may have some effect on students' progress in the L2 (see Flores, 1973, cited by Cohen, 1974). Generally, the immersion philosophy is not to *correct* errors but rather to model the correct response for the learners, as suggested in the *Immersion Teacher Handbook* (Snow, 1987: 22). One study found that adding emphasis to the corrections produced better results (Chaudron, 1983).

The teachers in our study handled errors in various ways, but were not particularly concerned with them (See Salomone, this volume). Sometimes errors were ignored (e.g. mispronunciation of vu as /vu/ rather than /vy/; 'content' used to describe girls, rather than 'contente'; /suriz/ for 'souris'; and 'anglais bibliothèque' accepted).

Most often, the teachers modeled the correct language:

(1) **Student:** 'peuvent' as /pøvã/

Elvina: '/pøv/'

(2) **Student:** 'Ce n'est pas triangle'. [This is not triangle.]

Elvina: 'Un triangle'. [A triangle.]

(3) **Student:** 'Pour practicer'. [To practice.]

Patrice: 'Pour pratiquer'.

(4) **Student:** 'Cent quatre-vingt et un'. [One hundred eighty and one.]

Patrice: 'Non, cent quatre-vingt-un'. [No, one hundred eighty-one.]

(5) **Student:** 'Mixé comme la soupe'. [Mixed (wrong word choice) like the soup.]

Marie: 'Mélangé comme une soupe'. [Mixed like soup.]

(6) **Students:** 'Present' (spoken as English)

Pierre: 'Présent, présent' (emphasizing French é)

(7) **Student:** '. . . poison . . '. [poison]

Denise: 'Regarde ma bouche: "poisson"'. [Watch my mouth: 'fish'.]

(8) **Student:** 'Mon maman'. [My mother.] (masculine article)

Nadine: 'Ma maman . . '. [My mother.] (feminine article)

(9) **Student:** 'J'ai tombé'. [I fell.]

Nadine: 'Je suis tombé'.

Students sometimes repeated the corrections spontaneously, but were requested to repeat at other times. Such suggestions as 'Tu peux le dire?' [Can you say it?] and 'Dis-le un peu en français' [Say it in French] were noted.

One teacher among the six in our study seemed to have a philosophy that differed from the traditional one of immersion: she attended to language *form* as well as to communicative language *use*. During modeling of corrections, she used the emphasis that Chaudron (1983) found effective: 'Je *me* suis trompé. Tu t'es trompé' [I was wrong. You were wrong.] Along with modeling of corrections, she often gave brief grammar-based explanations. When she wrote the correction, 'une planche,' on the board, a student asked her why she did not write '*un* planche'. Nadine responded:

'Il n'y a pas d'explication. C'est féminin et c'est *une*. There's no trick. You just have to learn it like that'. [There isn't any explanation. It's feminine and it's *une*.]

and

Student: 'Le petit rouge poisson . . '. [A little red fish . . .].

Nadine: 'Rouge vient après'. [Red comes after.]

and

Student: 'Je joue'. [I play.]

Nadine: 'C'est pas je, c'est j'ai. C'est passé. Ce n'est pas maintenant'. [It's not I, it's I have. It's past. It isn't now.]

Student: 'J'ai joué'. [I have played.]

The teachers at Glenwood School followed the immersion philosophy and schedule for 'early total immersion' (all French in kindergarten and grade 1, then one hour of English language arts in grade 2, increasing until grade 5 when the day is half French, half English). As a general rule, they corrected only by modeling, except for Nadine. Such seemingly simple additions to the 'programme' as the above grammar explanations may contribute effectively to students' grammatical competence.

Many now believe that an element of analytical teaching could eliminate immersion students' grammar deficiencies. Bibeau (1984) suggests that 'pure' immersion is *dépassé*; he encourages incorporating a period of intensive language teaching/learning into the immersion program—at least 1/3 of the total instructional time. Hammerly (1987) reiterates his plan for achieving bilingualism in students: an exploratory languages-of-the-world course followed by semi-intensive systematic language instruction, then partial immersion, and finally total immersion or submersion. An immersion teacher himself, Lyster (1990) advocates developing units around difficult grammatical structures as long as these units are integrated into functional or thematic contexts and maintaining the overall immersion program.

As Lyster suggests, Nadine, while maintaining the overall immersion program, included lessons on French grammar and phonics in addition to the above grammar explanations. She led a discussion of vowels, including vowel combinations, 'Quand on met les voyelles ensemble, ça change le son. OU—quels mots ont ce son?' [When we put vowels together, it changes the sound. OU—what words have this sound?] Students gave examples (*le cou, le coucou, des sous, beaucoup, bouger*), and the discussion continued with the sound of oi. When the example *doigt* was offered, Nadine asked how to spell the word, then asked why its spelling was difficult. A student answered, 'On n'entend pas le *t*'. [We don't hear the *t*.]

Nadine prompted, 'Et aussi?' [And also?] to which he added, 'On n'entend pas le *g*'. [We don't hear the *g*.]

Moreover, student questions about spelling were addressed by Nadine's asking them to 'sound out' the spelling during compositions. This practice was different from that observed in another classroom where students were told: 'Tu écris comme tu penses'. [Write like you think.]

Indications of grammar lessons included posters showing *être* and *avoir* verb conjugations, probably a basis for studying the past tense. Also, practice sentences with the conjugated verb + infinitive construction were written on the blackboard:

Nous faisons des phrases. [We make sentences.]

Je peux manger un gâteau. [I can eat a cake.]

Je peux jouer avec mon ami. [I can play with my friend.]

Il peut courir dehors. [He can run outside.]

Elle peut travailler et écouter dans la classe. [She can work and listen in class.]

Jon va marcher dans le métro'. [Jon is going to walk in the métro.]

Other direct references to grammar concerned the *passé composé*. Nadine raised student consciousness about grammar with the following comments:

(1) **Nadine:** 'Attention, c'est derrière nous, devant nous, ou maintenant?' [Attention, is it behind us, in front of us, or now?]

(2) **Nadine:** 'Quelle est la différence? Maman fait un bon gâteau ou Maman a fait?' [What is the difference? Mother makes a good cake or Mother made?]

Student: 'Already happened'.

Gender was also discussed by teacher and student in Nadine's room:

Nadine: 'Quelle est la différence entre le lapin ou la lapine? When it's a female— "femelle" ' [What is the difference between the (male) rabbit or the (female) rabbit?]

Student: 'lapine'.

Nadine: 'Quand c'est un mâle, c'est un lapin'. [When it's a male, it's a *lapin*.]

Student: 'Il y a un e à la fin quand c'est lapine—femelle'. [There is an *e* at the end when it's (female) rabbit—female.]

One must admit, from the multiple examples of student error cited herein, that grammatical inaccuracy does exist in immersion student speech. Slight modifications of the immersion process, however, may be able to help eliminate these errors. Examples from Nadine's phonics lessons and grammatical consciousness-raisings can provide models of one teacher's attention to *form* within the immersion context. Such minor adjustments in the immersion philosophy and practice may improve student grammatical competency.

Convergent Questioning Techniques: The Process

On the other hand, some of the charges directed at the immersion process may be unfounded. Lapkin & Swain with Shapson assert that 'teachers typically ask students fairly narrow questions where the expected answers are short and predictable' and 'such convergent questioning techniques limit the use of higher order thinking skills. . . (and) constrain the use of extended discourse on the part of the students' (1990: 654). It appears to be true that in language-oriented classes, such 'display questions' designed primarily to practice language are common. Long & Sato (1983), for example, found that teachers used significantly more display questions than referential (information-requesting) questions in their English as a Second Language classroom. Rulon & McCreary (1986) concurred, contending that little negotiation of meaning or content occurred in teacher- fronted classrooms.

At Glenwood School, however, display questions serve a definite pedagogical purpose. Teachers at this school are constrained by the local course of study to teach required content for each grade level. Teaching concepts, rather than language, is their primary goal. Display questions help teachers ascertain students' mastery or non- mastery of these concepts. These questions are not for the display of linguistic knowledge; they are an important part of content learning. It is only secondarily that language is practiced in the process. Content display questions at Glenwood may be

(1) a sentence-completion type:

Patrice: 'Il est tout '. ('seul') [He is all . (alone)]

Pierre: 'Dave est con . . '. ('content') [Dave is hap . . '. (happy)]

Pierre: 'Qui est content?' ('Dave') [Who is happy? ('Dave')]

(2) answered non-verbally: **Marie:** 'Montrez un peu les triangles avec les mains'. [Show triangles with your hands.] [first grade)

Estelle: 'Qui peut dessiner un menton?' [Who can draw a chin?] (fifth grade)

Patrice: 'Les clowns jouent de la trompette. Faites-le'. [Clowns play the trumpet. Do it.]

(3) short answer: **Patrice:** 'Quel jour est-ce?' ('mercredi') [What day is it? (Wednesday)]

Marie: 'De quelle couleur est le triangle?' ('jaune') [What color is the triangle? (yellow)]

Pierre: 'Le 31 octobre, c'est quoi?' ('Halloween') [October 31, what is it? (Halloween)]

Estelle: 'Quelle est la température?' ('soixante') [What is the temperature? (sixty)]

(4) dichotomous: **Nadine:** 'Le gâteau—un flan ou un gâteau au fromage?' ('un flan') [The cake—a flan or a cheesecake?]

Nadine: 'Qu'est-ce qu'on regarde d'abord—la petite ou la grande aiguille?' ('la petite') [What do we look at first—the little or big hand? (little)]

Patrice: 'L'éléphant se lave avec sa trompette ou trompe?' ('trompe') [The elephant washes himself with his trumpet or trunk? (trunk)]

(5) prompted by incorrect responses: **Nadine:** 'René et Jojo sont 2 filles?' ('2 garçons') [René and Jojo are 2 girls? (2 boys)]

Denise: 'Quel jour est-ce aujourd'hui? C'est lundi?' ('mardi') [What day is it today? Is it Monday? (Tuesday)]

Contrary to the comments made by Lapkin *et al.* that immersion teachers use convergent questions thereby limiting the use of higher order thinking skills and extended student discourse, at Glenwood School many instances of divergent questioning techniques were observed. Even Pierre, in kindergarten, often was observed asking 'Pourquoi?' [Why?] questions that students answered in English. By third grade, Patrice could ask such demanding questions and receive answers in French.

In addition to content display questions and higher-order questioning, teachers and students at Glenwood School communicated about topics that were meaningful to both groups. Gunterman & Phillips (1982) assert that the most real communication in the classroom is that which deals with classroom behavior. It follows that this communication would be inherently meaningful and a useful vehicle for second language acquisition. At Glenwood School much of this communication was observed:

To determine attendance—'Il y a des absents?' [Are there any absentees?] (grade 3)

lunch count—'Tu as un sac?' [Do you have a sack lunch?] (grade 5)

weather—'Est-ce qu'il y a un nuage ou beaucoup?' [Is there one cloud or several?] (grade 1) classroom directions—'On va s'asseoir à sa place' [Let's go sit in our seats.] (kindergarten)

lining-up activities—'Les filles qui portent un pantalon/ une robe/ une jupe. Les garçons avec les yeux bleus/ qui portent des lunettes/ qui portent des chaussures blanches/ qui portent des pantalons bleus' [Girls wearing pants/ a dress/ a skirt. Boys with blue eyes/ who are wearing glasses/ who are wearing white shoes/who are wearing blue pants.] (grade 3)

and assignments—'On va faire la page 6. Si la page 6 est finie, on va faire la page 7'. [We are going to do page 6. If page 6 is finished, we will do page 7.] (grade 1)

Teachers and students also discussed their personal lives outside school, a topic that also ranked in the 'real communication' category for Gunterman & Phillips (1982). The language of communication might be student English or French, but a considerable amount of information exchange was recorded. Journal-writing activities were always preceded by a discussion of what students were planning to record about their personal lives. Teachers asked questions about the school day's activities, students' weekends, their families, and their moods; and 'Pourquoi?' [Why?] questions often probed for more information while providing for extended student discourse.

According to Seliger (1983), students who initiate interactions must attend to their own output as well as to the response of the addressee. In so doing, they become more involved in their own language learning. Glenwood School students often initiated interactions with their teachers. Topics of these exchanges included reminders of the daily routine ('Faire les mathématiques maintenant?' [Do math now?]), offers to help ('Je peux passer les feuilles?' [I can pass the papers?] reports on other students' abilities ('Il parle français un petit peu' [He speaks French a little]), content corrections ('Tu as oublié 4 × 7' [You forgot 4 × 7]), comments on activities ('On pointe les pieds pour le ballet' [We point our toes for the ballet]), and questions about activities ('Si un sac tombe?' [If a bag falls?]).

The following vignette may give a clearer picture of elementary French immersion teaching as I found it at Glenwood School. Not only are many teaching techniques and teacher–student interactions represented, but also the expanded student discourse that Lapkin & Swain found wanting is vividly illustrated.

Patrice, a third-grade teacher, is beginning 'Casquettes à vendre' [Caps for Sale], a children's story that has been popular for several generations. She does not actually read the story, but rather explains it. She describes what a 'colporteur' is—'Il vend des choses porte à porte dans la rue' [He sells things door to door in the street] and 'casquettes,' which (she suggests by gesture) are worn 'Sur la ____' [On the ____] ('tête' [head], children answer). There are 17 casquettes. Patrice integrates math and language by having students count by four to see how many of each color there are—four grey, four yellow, four red, four blue, and one checkered ('à carreaux'), which she explains by saying 'Comme la robe de Jane' [Like Jane's dress].

Patrice continues, 'Il marchait dans la rue bien droit. Pourquoi est-ce qu'il se tient bien droit?' [He walked in the street very straight. Why did he walk so straight?] a higher-order question (see Barrett, 1972) that demands logical thinking. Next, she again forces the students to think, 'Pourquoi n'a-t-il pas d'argent?' [Why didn't he have any money?] One student offers, 'Il a acheté les casquettes'. [He bought the caps.] Another says, 'Personne ne vient pour acheter les casquettes'. [No one comes to buy the caps.]

The *colporteur* sleeps under a tree, and all but one of his caps disappear. Patrice asks students to imagine, 'Où sont-elles, les autres?' [Where are they, the others?] and they offer:

'Ils allaient dans le vent'. [They went in the wind.]

'Un singe vient et prendre le chapeau et mettre sur sa tête'. [A monkey comes and (to) take the hat and (to) put on his head.]

'Une personne vient vendre les casquettes'. [A person comes to sell the caps.]

'Dans la poche'. [In the pocket.]

'Il rêve'. [He is dreaming.]

When one student gives the story's answers, Patrice asks, 'Tu as lu le livre à la bibliothèque?' [You read the book at the library?] to which the student answers, 'Non, à la maison' [No, at home], and Patrice shows interest in a real information exchange by asking, 'Oh, tu as le livre à la maison?' [Oh, you have the book at home?]

Only one cap remains; Patrice suggests, 'Il ne reste que ____' [There is only ____] and a student answers, 'Un' [One], which Patrice corrects by modeling, 'Une casquette'. She then asks for non- verbal responses, 'Qui est-ce qui dit qu'il voit les casquettes dans l'arbre?' [Who says that he sees the caps in the tree?] and students raise their hands. Then she asks, 'Qui est-ce qui dit qu'il ne voit pas les casquettes dans l'arbre?' [Who says that he doesn't see the caps in the tree?], which is followed by another show of hands. After Patrice turns the page, the students see that monkeys have taken the caps and are wearing them as they hang in the tree. She has them all count the caps on the monkeys' heads. One student, however, argues with Patrice that there are 17, not 16, and must be convinced—evidence of student free expression.

Patrice now challenges their creativity. In response to the higher- order question, 'Qu'est-ce que tu ferais?' [What would you do?], the following answer was given by Jane:

'Tu peux prendre les singes et tu peux va dans la rue avec les singes et les singes va marcher derrière toi et les personnes va vient et va acheter les casquettes'. [You can (to) take the monkeys and you can go in the street with the monkeys and the monkeys (go to) walk behind you and the people (go) come and (go to) buy the caps.]

It goes without saying that this response, among others, provides clear evidence that extended student discourse can and does arise from divergent questioning techniques at Glenwood School.

Patrice continues, 'Qu'est-ce qu'il peut dire aux singes? Gentiment'. [What can he say to the monkeys? Nicely.] Students answer, 'Donne-moi les casquettes'. [Give me the caps.] Patrice, 'Il se met en colère. Il est ' (Students: 'fâché'.) [He gets angry. He is (Students: 'mad'.)] 'Il dit, 'Rendez-moi les ' (Students: 'casquettes') [He says, 'Give me the ' (Students: 'caps')]. 'Les singes disent ' (Students: 'Non!') [The monkeys say (Students: No!)] Patrice then asks, 'Qu'est-ce qu'il va dire?' [What is he going to say?] and evidence of agreement errors appears, 'Donnez- moi ma casquettes!' [Give me my (singular) caps!] Then, a newer student tries, 'Le man stomped la pied' [The (man stomped) his (wrong gender article) foot], illustrating both the insertion of English and gender confusion.

When the *colporteur* finally recovers his caps, a student offers (unsolicited), 'Tout est bien qui ..'. and Patrice finishes for her '... qui finit bien'. [All is well that ... that ends well.]

Conclusion

The *product* of immersion teaching, student achievement, has been studied extensively during the past 25 years. Researchers have found immersion students to achieve English language skills comparable to their English-language-educated age-mates (e.g. Barik & Swain, 1975; Lambert & Tucker, 1972; Swain & Lapkin, 1982). Their academic achievement in other subjects is also comparable (Barik & Swain, 1975; Genesee, 1983; Lambert & Tucker, 1972; Swain & Barik, 1976).

When compared with francophone students, immersion students seem to achieve as well in receptive French language skills (e.g. Cziko, 1978, 1980; Genesee, Holobow, Lambert, Cleghorn & Wallin, 1985; Lambert & Tucker, 1972; Pawley, 1985). One must acknowledge, however, that immersion students' productive skills lag behind those of their francophone peers (see Genesee *et al.*, 1985; Gray, 1986; Harley, 1984; Lambert & Tucker, 1972; Lapkin, 1984; Morrison & Pawley, 1986; Pawley, 1985). Grammatical errors are common in immersion students' speech and writing. Adding analytical language-study units and/or phonics and grammar consciousness-raising may help to eliminate them. Such focus on form could discourage deficiencies in the immersion *product*.

Certainly, less attention has been paid to the process of immersion teaching. Lambert & Tucker (1972), for example, devoted only six pages to descriptions of two-hour observations in each of the St. Lambert classrooms. Our study focused on the immersion process and the teachers who direct instruction in six immersion classrooms. Based on over 85 hours of intensive observation, data from our study provide evidence that some conclusions about the immersion process may need to be reconsidered. It is true that many display questions are used at Glenwood School. But, these are not the linguistic practice exercises common to second-language classrooms. They are, rather, verifications of concept learning—the primary goal of immersion teaching. Many instances of negotiated meaning—true communication—occurred among students and teachers at Glenwood. Moreover, divergent questioning techniques, which Lapkin *et al.* (1990) find wanting, were in abundance. As early as kindergarten, many examples of higher-order questions were observed.

Many agree with Krashen that French immersion is 'the most successful programme ever recorded in the professional language-teaching literature' (1984:61). At the same time, potential flaws in immersion education have received a great deal of scrutiny. In response, perhaps, to Stern's suggestion that scholars now question, 'Is the level of French . . . the best that can be attained in this type of program or could it be further improved?' (1978:847), many have responded that students' grammatical competence needs attention. In addition, some have questioned the process of immersion teaching, citing its lack of higher order thinking activities. By adding analytical units (similar to those we observed) and continuing higher-order questioning techniques (that we often found), these deficiencies may even be minimized.

Part 3
Preparing and Maintaining Staff for Language Immersion Classrooms

6 The Development of Immersion Teachers

ELIZABETH B. BERNHARDT and LESLIE SCHRIER

Introduction

One of the primary objectives of the project 'Toward a Prototype Training Model for US Immersion Teachers' (1988) was to develop a set of research-based guidelines for educating future immersion teachers; i.e. for preparing pre-service teachers to enter language immersion teaching settings and for helping experienced practitioners become immersion teachers. All of the components of this research project—that is, the Salomone study on immersion teacher behaviors, the work of Wilburn with drama, and the research of Hickman using authentic children's literature—pointed toward how to understand immersion teaching and how to translate it for future practitioners. This study reports the synthesis of findings from the research project into a prototype model for teacher development.

Historical Background

Research-generated guidelines for teacher preparation programs are rather uncommon. Bennett (1976) lamented this situation and was echoed by Biddle & Anderson (1986) when they stated: '...many teacher education policies are adopted without the benefit of research' (p. 248).

There have been, however, a few studies in which the findings from the research on teaching have been used to improve the instruction of inservice teachers. These studies (Anderson, Evertson & Brophy, 1979; Crawford *et al.*, 1978; Good & Grouws, 1979; Stallings, Needels & Stayrook, 1979) used research-based curricula in experimental inservice teacher education programs. The results of several of these experiments are reported by Gage & Giaconia (1981). Notably, in all of the experiments, teachers changed their behavior and student achievement was significantly affected.

Despite positive outcomes from studies such as those cited above, the principal impetus for developing programs from a research-base has been sociopolitical. In general, social changes in the past decades have required massive efforts to retrain teachers to help them work with mainstreamed handicapped students, multicultural student groups, recent immigrants, and low-achieving students. The avenue for educational improvement led directly through the schools, rather than indirectly through teacher preparation programs. The reasons for this policy were many: during the mid-1970s very few new teachers were being hired; fewer children were in schools and tenured teachers were staying in their jobs longer. Against these demographic factors, the 1980s found traditional educational institutions reacting to vociferous criticism found in documents such as *A Nation at Risk* (National Commission on Excellence in Education, 1983) and *Tomorrow's Teachers* (Holmes Group, 1986). These reports raised grave concerns about the nation's schools and the quality of teaching within them.

Accompanying the questions about the general quality of traditional educational institutions was a specific criticism of the foreign language competency of the nation's students. The catalyst for this criticism was a presidential commission report, *Strength through Wisdom, A Critique of US Capability* (1979). Developed during the Carter administration, the report emphasized how the nation's lack of competence in foreign language and international studies affected its economic competitiveness in an ever-expanding world marketplace. One of its many recommendations was for foreign language teachers 'to teach the spoken language more effectively' (p. 20).

One remedy recommended for improving the spoken foreign language skills of Americans was to establish foreign language instruction at the elementary school level. Drawing upon the Canadian response to social change and political demands, immersion schooling appeared to be an appropriate and effective model.

The creation of immersion schooling in the United States provided the American public education system with a new approach to educating the nation's students and, hence, created a new practitioner. The traditional curriculum of the elementary school was enriched by having its instructional activities delivered in a foreign language. The traditional elementary school teacher was changed into a practitioner who used a foreign language and not English as the medium of instruction. A traditional educational institution—the elementary school—changed by virtue of the language that was used in instruction.

The Study

The importance of a research-based curriculum for developing elementary foreign language teacher competencies was underlined over twenty years ago. In a status report of foreign language education in the elementary schools, Andersson (1969) comments on the need for a definition of competencies for foreign language elementary school teacher preparation:

> Educators have long struggled with this problem [a definition of teacher competencies], but perhaps from the wrong point of view. It is not necessary to form a comprehensive and philosophically consistent definition of a good teacher, but rather it is important to establish some simple working principles. For these principles ask the practitioner... (p. 176).

Twenty years after Andersson's statement little has changed. This project was in many ways a response to Andersson. Hence, the final component of the entire project was to ask experienced practitioners directly what kind of teacher education program they felt would most appropriately meet the needs of a developing immersion teacher. Rather than presuming to know how one becomes a successful immersion teacher, the researchers asked teachers, who had already gone through the process of becoming immersion teachers, what constitutes effective preparation (Hammadou & Bernhardt, 1987; Schrier, 1990).

The data collection had both an informal and a formal dimension. The informal dimension was characterized by side comments about 'what a teacher has to know' that were made in any phase of data collection—that is, in any of the sub-studies or in any debriefing sessions. The formal dimension consisted of structured interviews that specifically focused on how the Glenwood immersion teachers would prepare or would like future colleagues to be prepared as immersion teachers.

The informal phase

Informal is a synonym for serendipity. There were times throughout the two year study that the teacher-collaborators volunteered information about teacher development. In Salomone's study (this volume), teachers were asked about their preparation for immersion teaching. A reference to Salomone's cross-case combination data matrix indicates, however, that most of the teachers responded curtly to this probe with the exception of Denise (N = 5 responses) who was the most seasoned of all the teachers. Within those sets of responses to the two questions 'Do you think that this preparation [preparation you had for immersion teaching] was appropriate?' and 'What other preparation might have helped you?' there was one unequivocal response: more observation of immersion teaching. While all of the practitioners felt comfortable with their elementary school teaching preparation, they answered that they would have felt more secure with immersion teaching if they had observed more immersion teaching.

This finding is, however, a surprising one. As part of the study, the teacher-collaborators were financially supported to spend a school week with Canadian immersion teachers—observing and working with them. Of those who participated in the program with three different school districts in the Toronto and Montreal areas, only one reported that the observations were useful. More characteristic was this:

'The Canadian context is so different from ours—the children are better behaved and better able to handle school. We are not able to do the kind of group work we saw. While the techniques they use are good, we cannot use them here at Glenwood. They [Canadian teachers] are not told what to teach the way we are'.

The other teachers affirmed the statement, adding that they, too, saw little value in observing Canadian immersion teachers because the educational setting was so different. Specifically, the US teachers pointed to group work as a distinctive difference in the Canadian context.

From the discussion of the teacher-collaborators on the role of group work in an immersion setting, however, came some truly interesting comments regarding teacher education. The following is an illustration:

Teacher 1: I think that was what Patrice was saying to that kid who keeps saying: 'J'ai tombé' [I fell—incorrect auxiliary]. She's probably going to keep saying that to that kid. But in situations, eventually that kid's gonna hear Patrice say fifty times: 'Je suis tombée'.

Teacher 2: I had this child and she is one of my best students in French, and she is still saying: 'Je suis finie'. [I am finished. The correct form is 'J'ai fini'.]

? : Ah, oui.

Teacher 3: And that's the translation of an English structure.

Teacher 4: And it's something in my own room and I am screaming because I want to say to Danielle who is very good...she is translating more than the others, and she makes more mistakes with 'Je suis' and 'J'ai'. That's interesting.

Teacher 2: I've said it and I've said it. But I've never told them. I never got upset about it. I just: 'Oui, j'ai fini'. And the kids, they...and coming from other kids and not always me telling. I say: 'Eh, quoi? C'est à dire: "J'ai fini"'. And that's it. And she said it the right way. [Oh, what? That means: I'm finished.]

Teacher 5: Even...but...a young French speaking boy or girl would make the same kind of mistake. 'J'ai allé' and things like that. ['I went'— incorrect auxiliary]. It's a normal thing.

? : They say constantly...I hear: 'Je va'. [I 'goes'. The correct form is 'Je vais'].

Teacher 4: It's less open, isn't it?

Teacher 5: It's a normal thing. Oui, je veux dire 'tu prends' et 'je va'. Ils ne parlent pas comparablement.

?: You hear 'je va' now. [Yes, I mean 'you take' and 'I goes'. They're not speaking about the same thing.]

Teacher 3: You hear it in English. They'll say they 'taked' it instead of I 'took' it.

?: Ça viendra plus tard...la grammaire. Oui...ça viendra plus tard avec la grammaire. [That will come later...the grammar. That will come later with grammar.]

Teacher 5: Si, jusqu' à la troisième année de primaire. C'est normal. [It's normal right up to third grade in primary school].

?: Ah, oui. C'est très normal.

Teacher 4: 'Je suis fini' - Tu entends souvent ça dans une classe? [I am finished - do you hear that a lot in a class?]

?: Non, ça serait une traduction. Ça serait une vraie traduction. [No, that would be a translation...a real translation.]

Teacher 2: Je vais...je va. [I go...I goes]

?: Ce n'est pas de traduction. Je vais...je va...c'est leur façon de parler tout le temps...non, pas du tout. [It's not a translation. I go...I goes...it's their way of talking all the time...no, not at all].

Teacher 2: C'est plutôt la conjugaison et l'accord du temps. [It's more conjugation and tense agreement.]

?: Nous corrigerons la grammaire quand ils arriveront à l'école. On corrigera la grammaire, leur façon d'écrire. [We'll correct the grammar when they get to school. We'll correct their grammar, their way of writing].

Teacher 4: Mais pas trop tard oralement. [But not too late orally].

Teacher 2: Ce n'est pas une question de grammaire, d'apprendre la grammaire. C'est justement dans le temps il y a beaucoup d'oral et à un niveau plus élevé de conversation...un niveau plus élevé. Bon, les enfants...comme... parlent des choses au présent. Tous les enfants parlent moins du passé. Les temps en français sont plus difficiles à apprendre...le conditionnel et les choses comme ça. Quand on parle, on parle à un niveau plus élevé, on monte avec eux. Ce n'est pas d'apprendre les conjugaisons. Je pense que c'est une question de niveau de langue. [It's not a question of grammar, of learning grammar. It's just in tense, there's a lot of oral and at a higher level of conversation...a higher level. Children talk about things in the present. All children speak less in the past. The tenses in French are more difficult to learn, the conditional and things like that. When one speaks, one speaks at a higher level, and one goes up with them. It's not about learning conjugations. I think that it's a question of language level.]

Teacher 3: They're talking about Vygotsky and his zone of proximal development. It's judging the next level of sophistication...the ways like you said Mary...the next level of input.

Teacher 2: I think teachers need to know about these things.

The formal phase

At the end of the first year of data collection, all of the teacher- collaborators reacted and responded to the findings of the Salomone study. At the beginning of the second year of data collection, all of the participants viewed the video based on Salomone's study, *Immersion: The Double Challenge.* That video illustrated the category groups that Salomone had isolated in her data collection. As a result, the teachers had at least two formal opportunities to reflect on the behaviors that appeared to unify them as a group.

At the end of the showing of *Immersion: The Double Challenge,* the teacher-collaborators were asked if they would agree to be interviewed about teacher preparation within the context of the nine category groups. That is, they were asked if the research team could spend time with them as individual teachers in order to ask them whether they believe that the observed behaviors were 'trainable' and if so, in which manner future teachers would best be able to learn and develop such teacher behaviors.

The interview itself was, therefore, structured according to the following themes: *thematic units; organizational routine; visuals; gestures and body language; repetition; use of big books; discipline; peer teaching; teacher-centered teaching; sight word reading method; teachers' translations of student utterances; songs; self-image of students.* Each interview was begun with two general questions about this list of themes. First, how many of these characteristics come from within and how many are 'teachable?' Second, if you were to teach a methods course at a university, what would you do? What would the course consist of?

Within this structured context, individual teachers were interviewed for at least one hour. All of the interviews were transcribed, and using data analysis techniques similar to the ones used in the Salomone study for qualitative data, responses were tabulated and synthesized.

Structured Themes

Table 6.1 provides a tabulation of responses grouped according to the Salomone data. Only one category, organizational routine, that is, the explicit cuing of classroom activities in sequence, was considered by all of the teacher-collaborators to consist of knowledge that future teachers could be explicitly 'taught'. Other categories in which there was a fair degree of

Table 6.1 Teacher-collaborators' interview responses according to structured themes

	Yes	No
Thematic units	4	2
Organizational routine	6	0
Visuals	3	3
Gestures & body language	3	3
Repetition	2	2
Big books	5	0
Discipline	5	1
Peer teaching	1	3
Teacher-centered	4	2
Songs	2	2
Students' self-image	1	5

agreement were in the categories of 'discipline', the 'use of big books', and 'encouraging a positive student self image'. In the former categories, all of the participants, with the exception of Pierre, the kindergarten teacher, stated that they believed a course in classroom management and in discipline can be extremely useful and applied directly in a practical situation. Patrice provided a characteristic outlook:

> Well, discipline is very important. Especially in that type of setting, if they're not looking at you, they're not gonna get the message. So in a regular school if a child is not looking at you, he can still use his ear. But here, the child needs ears and eyes. So you need that discipline to be able to do that. Plus you have to have a kind of a routine. That way the children know exactly what's gonna happen next. They have to feel kind of safe inside a classroom with a certain pattern.

In like manner, all the teachers stated that the use of big books in an elementary classroom was extremely useful and that they had been helped by a number of teacher workshops on that topic.

In the final category of general consensus, encouragement of the individual child's self-image, almost all of the teachers believed that that particular teaching behavior was completely based on personality. Most of them noted that a teacher could not be taught to be a sensitive and caring person. Nathalie commented:

> It's a matter of having it or not. Because it's like the soul. People have it or don't have it in front of a painting or in front of something else.

You feel something or you don't...that's the capability inside of them to do it or not.

Marie was the only teacher who felt that potential teachers could parti-cipate in sensitivity training and could be made to practice positive encour-agement of each child's ability. She commented:

We can sensitize people about those things. Maybe if they understand what immersion teaching is, they can understand why or they can change themselves to be flexible and helpful...if you understand the goals, it's easier to make an effort and to try to change yourself.

Two other categories had a slight majority agreement: teaching by means of thematic units and keeping instruction teacher-centered. Four of the six teachers interviewed contended that introducing the concept of the integration of material across the curriculum would be an appropriate topic for teacher preparation. The discussion of this category was in fact the only time when any of the participants become extremely concrete. Each was able to describe how they would teach the concept of thematic unit. Marie, as one example, stated:

Maybe I can ask them to imagine the unit is the word 'green'. What can you tell me about the word 'green?' What do you think would be interesting to talk about this word 'green' which is not only a word, but which is a color....? I believe in the relationship between the different activities we are teaching in the classroom. So I would ask the student [teacher], how can you work with this unit? So ...if he or she tells me that green reminds them of plants, I can ask, what can you do with plants if it's in September? ...Let's say October...the leaves which are falling. And I will ask them what they can do in math with leaves...and I will ask the student [teacher] if she can make a group of vocabulary which can be useful for the different activities...

Two of the participants were fairly vocal in their opposition to trying to 'teach' future teachers how to use thematic units. Denise commented: 'I think you have to learn through experience and be in your classroom and see with the kids how you can do it. It's very difficult'. Later in the interview Denise responded to the question, could you teach a student teacher to set up an activity like that [an integrative lesson]? She replied: 'It comes from experience'. When asked again, she responded: 'No. No. You have to see everything...they [student teachers] have to learn that we integrate every-thing. That's all'.

Estelle replied with a similar spirit: 'You have a lesson. You have the objectives. You have the materials. You have the procedure. You have the methodology. You have this. You have that. You get in the classroom, and forget it. ...then you have to rely on your ability to ad lib'.

In the Salomone study, keeping instruction 'teacher-centered' means that teachers maintained control and were at the center of students' attention; that is, that little or no group or individual work was conducted. Again, four of the teachers believed that teacher-centeredness was an important concept that could be taught. They explained that new teachers have to understand that they are the only accurate models for language and that, therefore, they must maintain the attention of the students at all times. Patrice explained the rule she would present to new teachers:

You talk to them, and they look at you....I tell them all the time: look at my mouth and look at my eyes. That's what I want. And not move...and yes, there are sometimes when they can move, of course, but you are moving with them.

Marie presented the other view regarding instructing 'teach- centeredness' to pre-service teachers. She noted:

A lot comes from the child. Well, here in the immersion setting, it's going to come even if it's in English. The idea is still there. And as a teacher you use the idea to make your lesson actually. You start from the children.... And it's a lot more productive that way because if it comes from them, it means that they are interested in it. Instead of me pushing them in that direction that day, I am more going in their direction with what they ask me for, and the next day I can go back to the others, to the other things I had predicted to do...[Teachers] have to work on it and try to listen to children...and not to yourself doing all the talking.

The remainder of Table 6.1 indicates an evenly split opinion among the teacher-collaborators. Half believed that teachers could be trained in the use of visuals, gestures and body language, repetition as a comprehension device, translation to acknowledge a student's utterance, and of songs; half did not.

Unstructured Themes

There were, of course, other themes that emerged as the teacher- collaborators were being interviewed. These are listed in Table 6.2. The principal theme was that of integration. A count of all of the transcripts indicates that the word was used explicitly 37 times and implicitly any number of other times. In fact, one might say that the first generalization to learn about becoming an immersion teacher is that all classroom activities must be integrated. Second, there was a pervasive belief among these teachers that ultimately teachers learned to be effective teachers by watching other teachers. Each one of the respondents used the word experience at least three times. Some of the respondents were quite explicit about their disdain for training. Pierre, for example, said: 'Anything I had in college overseas

Table 6.2 Number of teachers mentioning other themes in the unstructured portion of the interview

Integration	6
Experience	6
Elementary school training	6
Language fluency	6
Child development knowledge	5
Relating to parents	4
Recognition of immersion workload	4
Personal immersion experience	1
Training in reflective teaching	1

or over here never helped me a lot. It was never very practical'. Nadine also remarked: 'You need to pass through different steps, and if you can see and do it yourself, it's probably the best way'. Estelle had similar thoughts: 'I might have a day when I actually see textbook children. I might have a day when I have a textbook lesson. I might, but then, most of the time I won't!'

Others did not speak directly to this point, but rather chose to refer to how important their practice teaching was. Each also offered that student teachers should have at least twenty weeks of full-time teaching experience, with Marie commenting: 'The more they stay in the classroom, the more they learn'.

Only one teacher, Marie, expressed belief in peer teaching. She said: 'And by asking the student teacher in the classroom to simulate that they are teaching to their peers could be good way of self-learning; but always with a theoretical teacher, a researcher, a professor, maybe, and maybe a teacher who knows what goes on in the classroom. All together...'.

When asked directly, however, what should be in an immersion teacher education curriculum, there was some remarkable consistency in their responses. All of them stated that they were primarily elementary teachers. In fact, all of the participants except for Estelle said they saw very little difference between immersion teaching and what they would do with native French-speaking children. Pierre admitted, though, that there were concrete things that he had to do that he would not have to do in a native speaking classroom. He noted:

Yes, I will need a big visual to show a grey crayon that I wouldn't need overseas, maybe, but some of the things we do in the classroom when we use visuals, when you use hands-on and all that, it's with the thought of just the way I would be teaching no matter of the setting.

Denise assented stating that she probably repeats more often in an immersion setting than in a native language setting.

All of the-participants also insisted that a teacher had to be completely fluent. Patrice explained that one of the reasons for the demanded fluency is that a teacher who had to stop to think of a word would not be able to integrate material from content to content and would keep the children up in the air. She continued:

> The first priority will be fluency; you have to be fluent. You can't just know a language, the basic of a language. You have to be completely fluent. If you're talking science, about things and everything, you have to be fluent. It's something you don't learn in a French course. Something you really need should be a person who has been living in the country, you know, for a while and be able to really speak about everything and each subject and everything like that.

In actuality, fluency was seen as a prerequisite to immersion teaching.

Most of the teacher-collaborators maintained that immersion teachers should be well-versed in child psychology. Denise explains:

> You need child psychology courses in the university where you have to understand that a seven year old child is not the same thing as an eight year old and the behavior is very different. At each level they [future teachers] have to understand that.

Another training aspect that was consistent across the interviews was the belief that immersion teachers should know immersion research. Denise commented:

> I read a lot of things so that it didn't seem so scary. ...It seems that if you don't speak English to the kids, I would be worried... And through my reading I see that their English skills are really sometimes higher than some regular classrooms. And this calms us down. That's why it's less scary.

Marie agreed:

> If you know theoretically what you are talking about, you can use that in a practical sense. And especially for a person who is twenty or twenty- three years old, with no experience, this is necessary to have basic knowledge about immersion teaching and to try to use that knowledge in the classroom.

Two final unifying themes across the interviews were parents and the immersion workload. All of the teachers felt that new teachers needed training in how to relate to parents. They explained that parents need special training in understanding immersion education as well as in how to help the children with their homework. Denise indicated:

Particularly in an immersion setting, the parents don't realize really that we teach in the language. They enroll their kid in the school, and sometimes they don't know why they did that...because it would be fun to learn French or...but they don't realize that it can be difficult and frustrating for the kids so you are constantly reminding the parents and sending letters. I send a newsletter every Friday to the parents explaining what I do, what my goals...

Researcher: So that would be important to understand that they have to establish...

Denise: A contact with the parents, a relationship with the parents constantly, and if there is a problem, call them.

Researcher: Would that be a high priority in something that you would discuss in a methods class?

Denise: Yes, absolutely.

In addition, all of the participants voiced the belief that future teachers really needed to develop an understanding of how much work is involved in immersion. Unlike regular elementary school teachers, immersion is more strenuous, has to be more teacher-centered because the teacher is the only resource, and materials are limited. All of the participants mentioned extended working hours particularly due to materials development demands.

Other facets of a potential teacher education curriculum were mentioned by smaller groups of individuals. One of the participants believed that anyone considering immersion teaching should be put through an immersion educational experience herself. One of the teachers stated:

They wanted us to feel what a person can feel when, you know, you don't know one word of a language. They chose Russian, and the person was talking a lot and not translating or anything and we were lost, and I mean that makes you feel really, you know, how the person can react, how the child for the first year, the first year or when the child's coming from another school he's just so lost, and how much it's important to him. You know because you expect that. So that's the kind of situation that makes you remember. I'll never forget that. It made me really realize how a person doesn't know, you know, language, and here you're talking all the time, all the time in that language. It's like you know you need a lot of support, visual and gestural and facial and all. And he was coming to me, and I was just like: 'What does he want?' I needed to see something.

Another believed that teachers can and should be trained in reflection. She noted:

> I've got this horrible monitor in my head, and I play back everything I've done for the whole day. And I do it at lunch time. I do it any time I have a free minute. And all of a sudden, something dawns on me like: 'Wow! You know I should have considered that at the moment or at that time'. You could teach people to think that way.

Validation

Subsequent to this data collection, four Canadian immersion teachers, two Anglophone and two Francophone, were asked to reflect on the interviews for cross-validation purposes from a more experienced group. All four argued strongly that the most appropriate preparation for an immersion teacher was an elementary teacher's training. In fact, one declared: 'An immersion teacher is 100% an elementary teacher'. Moreover, there was strong agreement that drama plays an important role and that immersion teaching is rather more intense than working in a monolingual setting. A final common view was that experience is the best preparation. Like their US counterparts, Canadian teachers felt that the more experience in genuine settings, the better.

The only real point of contention between the two sets of participants was the role of group work: the Canadian Francophones commented on the effectiveness of group work for all children. The Anglophone teachers, however, commented that group work can be problematic in an immersion setting. One of the teachers noted that she tries to avoid using groups because of the 'bad French' she hears.

In the process of data collection, the researcher's beliefs were structured not only by the teachers being interviewed, but by publications. Patricia Westphal's diary study (1989) provided additional external validity.

In parallel to Denise's comment above, Westphal remarks:

> I tell everyone now that teaching in an immersion program was the hardest thing I've ever done, and that is no exaggeration (p. 1).

Regarding all of the participants' views on teacher education, Westphal notes:

> Fortunately there were new-teacher workshops... But what was most fruitful was observing and talking to veteran teachers (p. 2).

Westphal also came to the same conclusion that all of the study participants held regarding their role as elementary teachers:

> It took me a while to realize that I wasn't there to teach French. I was there to teach reading and math and social studies and science and spelling and penmanship and citizenship... French was incidental (p. 5).

Westphal, too, uses the word integration in her diary. In noting the complexities of implementing an elementary curriculum written in English into French, she concludes:

> Finally I isolated the major points in each of the guides and tried to integrate them as much as possible (p. 6).

Other points made in the Westphal study compatible with the participant–teachers' views involved skills in the management of classrooms as well as administrative duties and a deep understanding of the elementary curriculum.

In conclusion, through the use of the three data sources—the formal and informal interview phases with the US teachers; the reactions of the Canadian teachers; and Westphal's study—a picture of immersion teaching developed. Based on these data sources the following prototype for the education of immersion teachers emerged.

A Prototype Model of Immersion Teacher Education

During the final throes of data analysis the Richards & Nunan (1990) volume, *Second Language Teacher Education*, appeared. This book provided the researchers with additional insights, particularly regarding a micro versus macro approach to teacher education. Richards would label this project a micro approach to research on teaching. He describes this research as an analytical one that looks at teaching in terms of its directly observable characteristics; it looks at what the teacher does in the classroom. Richards juxtaposes this with the macro approach. The macro approach is described as holistic and that it 'involves making generalizations and inferences that go beyond what can be observed directly in the way of quantifiable classroom processes' (p.4).

Hence the model outlined here flows from the micro-level research into a proposed macro-level teacher development program. In line with current thinking, the model is based on a holistic approach to the study of teaching and the development of teacher preparation programs. It stems from Richard's (1990) belief in '...the examination of the total context of classroom teaching and learning in an attempt to understand how the interactions between and among teacher, learners and classroom tasks affect learning' (p. 9).

Using this holistic approach, the data indicate a dual-tracked system: one focused on a knowledge base developed through formal coursework; another focused on a knowledge base developed in field settings. Outlining such a program is not to suggest that one phase precedes the other or that they are in any way hierarchically arranged. In fact, the concept of prototype is critical. Prototype implies essential features only—not the only features.

Pre-requisites

The data indicated that pre-service immersion teachers must possess two qualities before engaging in immersion teacher development. The first is that the teacher possess native or near-native fluency in the target language. From Salomone's study, *Immersion: The Double Challenge*, and from the diary study by Westphal, the necessity for the teacher to be fluent in the target language was underscored. The practicing immersion teachers expressed concern for the preservice teacher who did not have sufficient facility in the language. They felt it was essential for the immersion teacher to be able to have the target language flow naturally during the execution of the lesson. Any hesitancy could ruin the intent of instruction.

Secondly, it is assumed that the preservice teacher must be prepared as an elementary school teacher. This assumption is germane to the situation of instruction: the elementary school. Previous definitions of immersion language programs in the United States fail to delineate the instructional responsibilities of the immersion language teacher as an elementary school teacher. They prefer emphasizing techniques for teaching isolated language modalities without emphasis on the use of the target language as the means of delivering the prescribed primary school curriculum (e.g. Curtain & Pesola, 1988; and Lipton, 1988).

Interactive experiences

The model proposed here for educating future immersion teachers has been developed through introspective research methods. It was extracted from the areas that the teacher-collaborators emphasized as essential in the preparation of future teachers. In listing these essential areas, it was discovered that the areas that would normally involve university-based preparation (e.g. developmental psychology or curriculum design) interacted naturally with experiences found in the actual immersion classroom.

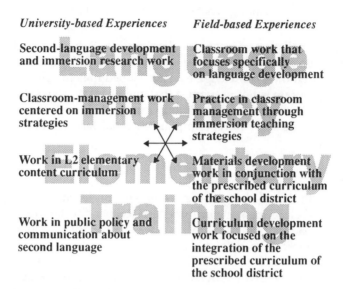

University-based Experiences	Field-based Experiences
Second-language development and immersion research work	Classroom work that focuses specifically on language development
Classroom-management work centered on immersion strategies	Practice in classroom management through immersion teaching strategies
Work in L2 elementary content curriculum	Materials development work in conjunction with the prescribed curriculum of the school district
Work in public policy and communication about second language	Curriculum development work focused on the integration of the prescribed curriculum of the school district

Figure 6.1 A prototype training model for US immersion teachers

Figure 6.1 illustrates the components of the model. Target language fluency and elementary school teacher preparation are the background qualifications necessary in order for preservice teachers to maximize their professional preparation. Formal experiences that the teacher-collaborators felt were pertinent to the preparation of immersion teachers are placed against this backdrop. Experiences are designed to help the teacher develop knowledge in various dimensions. Some of the knowledge can be gained through intellectual means, commonly known as 'training' in a formal educational setting. Yet, a real understanding of this clinical knowledge can only be gained through field experiences in the immersion classroom.

The heuristic used to organize the interactive experiences mentioned by the teachers was that of the immersion language classroom. For an immersion teacher to be an effective teacher, knowledge of the physical, emotional, and psychological development of the elementary school student should be part of the immersion teacher education curriculum. The immersion teacher will be teaching 'something' to the elementary student and that 'something' is the elementary school *curriculum*. Furthermore, the teacher will be teaching in a milieu that is markedly different from that of a foreign language or elementary school classroom, and that immersion school *environment* should be experienced as part of the preparation of the immersion teacher.

University-Based Experiences

The first dimension of the university-based coursework should focus on interactions with immersion students. Providing the preservice teacher with knowledge of classroom management strategies as well as instructional activities appropriate for the elementary school student was expressed frequently in both the Salomone study (e.g. Table 1.7) and the personal narrative by Westphal (1989). These competencies may seem self-evident in elementary school teacher preparation programs. They are, however, more complex when the medium of instruction is a foreign language. Teachers must acquire particular classroom management skills in a language that the children do not fully comprehend. In addition, these management skills must be compatible with both the home and the target culture.

The pre-service immersion teacher must also be prepared through coursework that emphasizes the elementary student's language development. Exposure to information on how, when, and in what manner, the child acquires the first language as well as second language communicative skills is essential to teacher development.

The second dimension of university-based coursework focuses on the elementary curriculum. Westphal (1989) realized midway through her teaching experience that above all the immersion teacher is concerned with presenting the elementary school curriculum to the students using the foreign language as the means of instruction and not as the goal of instruction (p. 6). The assumption is that the preservice teacher must have extensive knowledge about elementary school curriculum design. This knowledge is efficiently developed through coursework in elementary school teacher preparation programs. Knowledge of how to construct learning activities within the core curriculum is available, as well, through teacher preparation courses.

The third dimension is knowledge about the educational environment. Developing good communication skills is seen as a competency necessary in an effective immersion teacher. This competency is necessary to communicate with the home of the immersion students as well as with administrators and supervisors within the school district.

The practicing immersion teachers emphasized the need for the teacher to develop extraordinary communication skills with the parents of his/her students. Because the language of instruction in the classroom is necessarily different than that of the student's home, it was seen as necessary for the immersion teacher to be expert in explaining the goals and activities of the immersion program frequently and creatively. Common activities, such as, helping the child prepare for a spelling test cannot be done by the care-giver. Because of this, frequent communication about what does go on in an immersion classroom and how the student could be encouraged at home must be communicated to the student's care-giver.

The teacher him/herself must be able to explain the immersion teaching situation to others in a manner that might be of use in helping promote a greater understanding of immersion language instruction. Administrators, supervisors, and teacher educators need to be educated about the unique teaching situation the immersion classroom creates.

Field-Based Experiences

The first dimension of the field-based experiences also focuses on students. Applying knowledge of first and second language acquisition research in the creation of instructional activities for the elementary school immersion student was seen as knowledge that could be developed in the inservice immersion teacher. This knowledge would help the teacher determine the types of second language learning that could be expected from a typical elementary student. Hence, knowledge of first and second language development applied to specific learning activities and an understanding of what could be expected from the student would facilitate and improve immersion instruction.

Curriculum is the second dimension of the field-based immersion experiences. Three areas in the development of immersion teachers in relation to knowledge of the instructional curriculum were mentioned by the Glenwood immersion teachers and Westphal (1989). These areas all related to the integration of instructional activities throughout the curriculum. There was a need to understand how to develop materials to augment specific instructional activities, to review specific target language nomenclature germane to specific learning activities, and to integrate all of these elements by using a variety of instructional techniques. The practicing immersion teachers felt that techniques in executing an immersion instructional curriculum needed to be experienced in the field and then developed as the teacher gained experience.

The third dimension of the field-based experiences focuses on the school environment. Field experiences in the environment of the immersion school were mentioned as mandatory by all of the teachers interviewed by Salomone. The Glenwood teachers felt that there were certain instructional and classroom management techniques that were unique to immersion settings. Purposeful observations of these techniques, for example, watching how the teacher requires the students not only to listen to instructions, but to watch the teacher while listening to him/her give directions, would provide the preservice teacher with skills to aid the transition from preservice to inservice immersion instruction. A full semester field experience was considered to be absolutely critical.

As Figure 6.1 illustrates, the experiences are conceived to be interactive, with formal coursework informing the field experiences and vice versa. That is, formal coursework should present preservice teachers with questions and theories that are then researched within the field settings. At the same time, work on materials and curriculum development within the context of particular school districts and under the direction of experienced teachers should provide data and discussion for formal coursework in curriculum and classroom management.

Figure 6.1, as a prototype, only includes experiences that the majority of teacher-collaborators mentioned as essential to teacher development. Other experiences mentioned, including personal immersion experiences, coursework in drama, and practice in reflective teaching, could probably play a useful and constructive role in the development of an immersion teacher.

In addition, Figure 6.1 provides only the broadest outline of a teacher development program. It is, of necessity, broad. Foreign language teacher development programs must be responsive to the unique contexts in which they are situated—from large universities with a wealth of support staff to small colleges—and to their unique student populations. Each program type with its individual clientele must take any prototype and form it to its own needs.

Conclusion

Teacher development is a complex and intense process. Educational research has not found a totally satisfactory model of teacher development that is responsive to the complexities of teaching and, at the same time, cost-effective.

The prototype outlined here is one attempt to capture a model of teacher development from research. On the one hand, it suffers from a lack of data because it was developed from one group of teachers in a particular American inner-city context. But, on the other hand, it is data-based making it unique among foreign language teacher development models. Additional work with teachers in a variety of contexts—including different languages, different school situations, and teachers trained in a variety of educational settings—must be conducted in order to validate and enhance the prototype's development.

7 Meeting the Challenges of Immersion: The Role of the Foreign Language Supervisor

DIANE F. GING

Introduction

With a great deal of attention focused on global studies and international perspectives, foreign language study has once again become an important part of the American school curriculum. How does a foreign language supervisor convince a district to add total immersion schools? Considering the many problems that require solutions on a daily basis, why would a foreign language supervisor want to add immersion? There is one answer: because of the compelling evidence of the effectiveness of such schools (Campbell, Gray, Rhodes & Snow 1985). This evidence led me to the most challenging of all tasks I undertook as foreign language supervisor for a public school district: planning and implementing two elementary foreign language immersion schools.

A Brief History of the Immersion Program

The late 1970s and entire 1980s signaled a time for re-examination of American schools. Most large, urban districts had undergone or were threatened with court-ordered busing; unanticipated long-range implications of busing or threatened busing within such school districts left them, generally, in a state of decline. Most urban districts were suffering from 'white flight' as middle class clientele left for the suburbs due to 'white resistance to participating in racially balanced schools' (Ascher, 1985). In addition, the move toward zero population growth of the 1960s and 1970s brought a severe reduction in the number of school-age children. Hechinger (1981) notes that 'like all other aspects of American life, education

[was] sharply affected by the end of growth'. Schools were faced with new dilemmas they had not had to consider before.

Coinciding with this general period of time, and as a sharp counter-reaction to the 'relevant curriculum' of the 1970s, there appeared several national reports to address the general decline in quality and lack of public confidence in American public schools. Also during this same period of time, there was a pervasive feeling that the United States was losing its place as a world leader due to political and economic realities reflecting a lack of global-mindedness. Two reports in particular, *The President's Commission on Foreign Language and International Studies* in 1979 and *A Nation at Risk* in 1983, cited a woeful lack of international perspective and foreign language study as an important part of the curriculum. In *Education Agenda for the 1980s,* Hechinger (1981) reiterated the need to prepare youngsters to master foreign languages, pointing out that 'even as schools seek to create a sense of common purpose, they must help young Americans make new connections with the world beyond the US'.

A combination of these forces, then, was the impetus for the appearance, on a rather large scale, of a number of magnet or alternative schools in many school districts across America. As Ascher (1985) suggested, the growing enthusiasm for magnet schools as a strategy for both school improvement and desegregation came at a time when there was a height-ened mix of confidence and despair regarding the public schools. McMillan (1980) stated that magnet schools have almost always been used to avoid or somehow deflect court-ordered desegregation efforts. Magnet schools were designed to give parents schools of choice rather than schools of compulsion, a decision often taken away from them with the appearance of busing, and to attract and keep middle class families in urban school districts, making them so attractive educationally that these parents would want to enroll their children voluntarily (Foster in Ascher, 1985). Magnet and alternative school programs hit an all-time high in the 1980s with their existence in virtually every state in the nation (McMillan, 1980).

The public school district in which I worked suffered from all of the symptoms described. The district served some 68,000 students in the mid-1980s, down from a high of 110,725 students in 1971. Thus, many schools had been closed. Busing to achieve court-ordered desegregation had progressed smoothly, thanks to efforts from everyone in the city—but not without a toll on the schools. School leaders anticipated being released from court-ordered busing, so in an effort to make dramatic changes within the district, they began planning in 1984–85 new initiatives to revitalize the district's 120-plus schools. Although the district had already implemented a very successful alternative school program, the general consensus was that it could easily be expanded; interest from parents was clearly there. In addition, the success of several other programs in nearby large, urban districts spurred the district to consider expansion of its alternative program.

Among popular magnet programs were those which offered foreign language study to elementary school children, (FLES). FLES is an umbrella term used to describe foreign language in the elementary school within four general program types: FLEX, FLES, intensive FLES and immersion. Following a preliminary study in our district, a list of possible program options was drawn up, with foreign language immersion as one of the options. In this study, it was noted that immersion, in fact, had been tremendously successful in Canadian schools for some 15–20 years at that point.

Immersion was neither experimental nor untested. Yet, it was also clear that the political realities of Canada, a bilingual nation threatened by secession of one of its language groups, would not necessarily translate into an environment for successful language immersion programs in the United States. In addition, while the district sits in a relatively large city with a well-educated population, the city itself could hardly be considered cosmopolitan or international in scope. It is interesting to note, therefore, that there was neither a specific political nor geographical reason nor was there a grass-roots effort to begin foreign language immersion schools in my district.

Fortunately, a nearby city had already implemented a very successful foreign language component in their elementary magnet program in response to desegregation suits which were pending. In fact, the foreign language magnets were the most popular option in that city with 10 elementary schools devoted to these programs. Not all of the FLES programs were immersion programs; in addition, the immersion programs were *partial* immersion while we had decided to pursue *total* immersion. Visits were easily accomplished; the impressive immersion program in our neighbor's district was responsible, in part, for total immersion being written into our plan.

During 1985–86, serious study had begun in earnest in order to progress with plans for the expanded magnet program. The elementary expansion was led by an upper-level administrator who established task forces and additional committees to study the plan and make specific recommendations. At the same time, there was to be a smaller expansion of the secondary alternative program which would give attention to continuing programs begun in the elementary alternative programs. This expansion was led by a different upper-level administrator.

Personal experience has been that administrators are somewhat intimidated by foreign language programs, the result of which is to turn over the responsibility to the foreign language specialists. Therefore, the task forces and committees relied heavily upon my advice and my direction in spite of the fact that I was new in my job. At this time, I had begun reading extensively about immersion programs and immersion research and made trips to visit nearby immersion schools. I had to transform myself from someone with virtually no knowledge base about language immersion to someone who could be an informed and outspoken advocate for such programs, who could plan an effective program anticipating needs and roadblocks as they occurred, and who could provide solutions to problems that would occur.

Under the direction of the chair of the elementary expansion, I pursued the feasibility of one Spanish and one Japanese total immersion school. Spanish as a language of importance in the United States was an obvious choice. Japanese seemed to be a wise and forward-looking choice; a nearby car manufacturer had already attracted a number of Japanese businesses. The potential for needing a work force well-trained in Japanese language and culture seemed clear. I met with professors of Japanese at the local university in order to draw up a rationale and to discuss how to staff such a school. I investigated sources for materials, reporting back to the chair regularly. While I followed many of the same procedures for the Spanish school, it was immediately apparent from many different directions that the idea of a Spanish school was more readily and widely supported; staff and materials were much more readily available, too.

Meanwhile, district personnel consulted on other issues regarding the feasibility of the various planned schools, including which buildings could be reopened or revamped in order to meet the needs of the program and the community. Each immersion school was to have its own building, rather than being established as a program within an existing school. We felt we could support two language immersion schools and that the benefits of having each housed in its own building were clear. If the desire was to create a total immersion program, then it was imperative to have a total environment to support the program. A program which exists as a school-within-a-school also faces additional problems with different rules and regulations for different groups of students and staff within one building (Smith, Burke & Barr, 1974). There was a mixture of excitement and terror, euphoria tempered with nervousness, as each progressive step carried planners back to the drawing board with new considerations and new directions to follow.

During the summer of 1986, the plan was ready for presentation to the district superintendent and his cabinet for final approval to proceed. Many individuals were involved; one by one we would be asked to present the proposal whose development we led. Preliminary sessions were scheduled with several individuals in the district, serving as a practice or rehearsal. I learned what kinds of questions to anticipate, and framed responses or else determined where I needed to prepare more fully in order to frame appropriate responses. There were hours of preparation and study for what would become one of the most important presentations of my career!

The superintendent had a reputation for instinctively knowing when one was not adequately prepared and for unrelenting interrogation directed at any presenter in that situation. My studying and preparation paid off. As anticipated, there was strong resistance to the Japanese proposal; I found especially surprising the resistance from a Japanese American who was a member of the cabinet. When it seemed evident that the Spanish school would receive a go-ahead while the Japanese school would not, I offered, as almost an off-hand remark, that we could implement a French immersion school. The two immersion schools, one Spanish and one French, were accepted without further discussion. At that point, I had not investigated staffing or materials for a French immersion school at all— French had not even been in consideration. Thus the total immersion program in my district was begun.

Planning for the Immersion Program

The Fall of 1986 was spent in further refining proposals. School sites had been selected and plans were progressing with time lines for selecting principals and staff, for material preview, for staff inservice, for curriculum development, for recruitment of students. Support staff and budgets were proposed as projections for enrollment were established. During these months, too, we began to visit already established immersion schools and to make national and international contacts with immersion educators.

In January of 1987, committees were formed to select principals for the various new schools which were to be established. As a part of the interview teams for the principals of the French and Spanish schools, I actively pursued two candidates who had expressed interest. The contacts established over the previous months played a key role. A phone call to another city provided me with a list of possible interview questions for immersion principals. Our committee met to develop interview procedures, including the formulation of questions and optimal answers which we sought. By the first of February, the two principals were selected.

The principals and I worked almost non-stop from this point forward. Ultimately, we all still had our 'regular' jobs to contend with while developing the two new schools. At the same time, too, an international studies/foreign language emphasis middle school was to be implemented. A great deal of my time and attention had to be devoted to development of this school as well. The principals and I developed time lines for every step. The chair of the alternative school expansion committee was forceful in getting plans underway and accepted; she had since retired. Her replacement worked diligently with us. While the new chair oversaw many committees to develop these new schools with unique and complex needs, among them a Montessori school, she was very comfortable in dealing with the immersion schools, as second language acquisition was one of her areas of specialization. However, with thirteen new elementary magnet schools to develop, she relied on our advice a great deal.

One of the greatest challenges came in the form of a decision from on high: we would open both schools with all grades, K-5, rather than opening with grades K and 1 and building with each progressive year. We had to design a program that made educational sense and had to delineate how each grade would look in successive years as the program evolved into total immersion. Our lack of experience made us hesitate to begin early and middle immersion all at once.

The three or sometimes four of us spent a good deal of our time, initially, making visits to other districts in order to become as informed as possible on virtually every aspect of immersion. It was at that time that we developed certain strong beliefs which would guide the development of our schools. We benefited greatly from the experiences of others who were more than generous in spirit and in fact. Riordan (1972) noted that in order to develop a successful program, schools should establish communication networks with other alternative schools, and to share experiences with each other. We spent time observing classes, talking to parents, administrators, teachers, supervisors, aides—in short, anyone connected in any way with an immersion program. Some of the visits were accomplished on our own time and at our own expense, such was our commitment to developing the best possible schools. In addition, the time spent with the newly selected elementary principals was tremendously helpful for me, a secondary-trained educator who needed a crash course in elementary school philosophy and practice. Becoming an expert on immersion requires expertise in elementary school pedagogy, including a solid understanding of child development as other articles in this book have documented.

Simultaneously, we moved ahead with our student recruitment plan. The district's Communication Department was helpful as we developed a slick brochure to market the schools. We targeted day care centers, creating attractive flyers with information about parent meetings to learn more about French and Spanish immersion school opportunities. We also left flyers at area libraries, churches, shopping malls, and medical offices. In addition, our local newspaper sent reporters to observe total immersion schools in other cities first-hand. The result was a comprehensive story on immersion education with information regarding the impending opportunity in our district.

The district scheduled a series of informational nights where all alternative schools were presented: a shopping mall of ideas for parents! On our own, we also scheduled parent information meetings about immersion on several different evenings and at several different sites around the city. As with all alternative schools within our district, all students would be eligible to attend. Children are not screened for immersion; the only criteria for admission are the interest and involvement of parents and racial balance. Free transportation is provided from any part of the district to alternative school sites, making the schools accessible to virtually any child who resides in our district. This was, indeed, our test. The two immersion programs had no student population assigned to them. If we could not attract clientele, we would not be able to establish these schools.

For each presentation, we showed a video tape of another city's immersion schools. We also set up a very brief demonstration immersion lesson which we performed with the young students who were in the audience. It was compelling evidence when parents saw their children functioning in and responding to another language in a matter of minutes; children understood and reacted as we had known they would. We used an early draft of 'Twenty Questions: The Most Commonly Asked Questions About Starting an Immersion Program', subsequently published by Met (1987), as well as other relevant publications from our vast readings and studies, many generously suggested and provided by host districts during our visits.

We were successful in getting many parents at these meetings. Some came back again and again, to listen and to learn. We kept daily tabs on the number of students enrolling. While the numbers were small, the interest was there! We would, in fact, have an immersion program.

As numbers firmed up, we were able to make allocations for teachers. Job postings were published. We had sufficient interest from the public as a result of good publicity about the schools and from persons serving on advisory committees to have established a small list of teachers interested in applying for immersion school positions. Some candidates, however, had no idea what expectations were as far as language ability and certification. The two principals and I had come to consensus: we sought teachers with elementary certification and native or near-native language proficiency in French or Spanish. Much to our dismay, many of the secondary teachers we had hoped to cultivate proved to be ill-prepared for immersion teaching, either due to insufficient language proficiency or lack of confidence and training in teaching content (i.e. math, science, social studies,) as defined by our district's adopted Course of Study. On the one hand, we had many elementary teacher applicants who falsely believed that their year of foreign language study in college would suffice for teaching in an immersion program!

We formed committees for interviewing teacher applicants. Again, we conferred with other districts for possible interview questions and qualifications for successful candidates. Among the committee, we invited a professor from the local university to help assess language skills of candidates who were not native speakers. This individual had substantial experience with oral proficiency interviews, and also with immersion as a former district foreign language supervisor, former assistant superintendent and immersion parent. We had many applicants; Spanish positions were quickly filled, many with native speakers who were elementary trained. French positions were not being filled. It was now the end of March; we had hoped to have all teachers selected at this point.

Finally, we established contact with a Belgian resource person in Louisiana. One principal was given permission to make a recruiting trip to Louisiana where he interviewed several Belgian teacher candidates who had indicated an interest in coming to our district. He was able to observe some of these teachers in their actual classrooms. As a result of the trip, we were able to identify staff for the French immersion school; hiring them, however, was another matter.

At this point, I learned a great deal about immigration, visas, and foreign nationals wishing to work in the United States. It became clear that filling out 'routine government forms' was beyond the expertise of several administrators gathered in one room; we were clearly not equipped to handle the complexities of visas. Rather than waste further time and effort, we decided to hire an immigration attorney. While the price was high, it was certainly no higher than the combined salaries of the group of administrators who had attempted to fill out the forms originally—and who would have completed forms incorrectly, ignoring other requirements for obtaining the appropriate visas. We hired the same attorney that another district had used; we felt that her familiarity with what was needed would save us time and expense in the long run. We had to make several trips and had to send by overnight mail a number of documents on a rather regular basis. We were in constant touch with the Belgian teachers in Louisiana to obtain documents and other necessary papers we needed to forward.

We were also required to work closely with the State Department of Education in order to secure temporary teaching certificates. The amount of time and paperwork which had to be filed—and interpreted—was as incredible as was the amount of time and paperwork needed to obtain visas. We had begun the process in late spring and feared that we would not be able to begin school at the end of August because we lacked the proper credentials.

The teachers arrived in the early summer. On the humanitarian side, we helped them find housing and establish accounts with the school credit union. Drivers' licenses and automobile registration had to be obtained, too. The excitement began to build once again as we all worked together and got to know one another. The personal level of involvement with the Spanish immersion teachers was much less; they had been, for the most part, residents of our city and did not require the constant attention that the Belgian teachers required. Their interest level, however, was every bit as high. We spoke often on the telephone to calm and encourage one another.

We had requested and received supplemental summer hours for curriculum development and pre-service for the staffs of both schools. The teachers remained under my direction, working on projects suggested by the principals who were off-duty during the summer. The French principal traveled to Lyon, France, as a part of an intensive study group while the Spanish principal hired a tutor in Spanish to strengthen his language abilities. This was yet another example of their commitment to the immersion program.

Teachers from both schools worked together to create a philosophy and program goals. We studied, at length, the district's Adopted Course of Study. From there, we scoured publishers for texts which could be used for the program, previewing many books, matching their content with the course of study and determining appropriateness in terms of student age level and potential language ability. We also worked diligently with field librarians to select appropriate books for the school libraries and ordered supplies and teaching materials for both schools. Since one of the schools was to be located in a facility that had been closed, there were some differences in funding allowances and needs.

At this point, plans were finalized for pre-service. Only a few of the teachers had immersion or bilingual teaching experience. The others demonstrated all ranges of expertise in second language acquisition theory;

most were trained as elementary teachers. We had a full week of intensive workshop activity led by a number of well-known immersion experts. Each day's activities were different and designed to provide a strong introduction to immersion teaching concepts. The additional challenge in the week of workshops was language itself. Some of the teachers were unable to comprehend totally some of the highly complex discussion which took place in English. When we tried practice demonstration lessons, the two language groups served us well; Spanish teachers were forced to make language comprehensible to the French language teachers and vice versa. This was truly immersion training!

There was a great deal of attention paid, in the workshops, to developing a thorough understanding of commonly-referenced immersion terms and concepts such as negotiation of meaning, comprehensible input, silent period, content-embedded and content-reduced language. We talked about second language acquisition theory and key instructional concepts and strategies for immersion classrooms (Curtain & Pesola, 1988). Teachers tried to experiment in conceptualizing actual lessons: which vocabulary words would be absolutely essential to the lesson; which words would be frequently used so as to become an active part of the vocabulary; how would teachers introduce abstract concepts which lacked any visual or concrete representation; how would teachers accomplish frequent comprehension checks; how would testing be accomplished initially, especially when students knew little of the second language.

In addition, we worked together to develop a definite plan for each grade level. Since the schools were to open with all grades, K-5, we had to define the program as it was phased in. After much reading and study, we decided to develop a three-year plan in which the upper grades would not participate in true immersion, but would have second language instruction more closely resembling a content-enriched FLES program. We looked carefully at percentages of time, divisions within the school day and particular subject areas which would lend themselves, more easily, to immersion principles and practices (Curtain & Pesola 1988). Strong commitment was developed to the concept of 'bilingualism through monolingualism' (Cummins & Swain 1986). As Gaarder (1978) also suggested, 'Keeping the two languages separate is fundamental to the child's later control and conception of them as separate systems representing distinct cultures'. We worked to reach consensus on what was acceptable in relation to children's use of English in the schools. We brainstormed ways to deal with discipline, with initial school safety issues, with classroom visitors, with parents, all designed to preserve and protect the total immersion classroom. We studied tips for parents and selected ideas and models from other immersion schools to develop an Immersion program Parent

Guide. Due to the phase-in nature of the program, the guide had to be updated each year for three years. We grappled with the problem of substitutes, of calendar deadlines and grade level limits for entrance into the program, of report cards and advisory committees. All of the planning and discussion continued without final legal approval to bring the Belgian teachers on board. At the last minute, visas were approved; opening day was upon us.

While we did receive visas in time for teachers to begin the school year, we also had a traumatic experience which almost prevented the issuance of the visas and would cause us difficulties for the next few years as well. Another district in a different state had initiated a rather ambitious magnet school program at this same time. Many of their magnets were foreign language school magnets of various program models. It was clear, however, that staff for all of these programs would not be available locally to this particular district; therefore, they recruited teachers from three foreign countries. The district filed legal papers without benefit of an attorney. Their visas were not approved. Unfortunately, the matter called disproportionate attention to our district that had successfully obtained visas and temporary teaching certificates for foreign teachers. As a result, there was some discussion that the visas might be revoked just after they were issued. At any rate, we were on notice for the following school year that it was likely that visa renewal would not occur. The visa question continued to plague the program, so much so that the district's Department of Teacher Personnel adamantly fought future attempts to pursue other foreign nationals.

Program Implementation

In 1987, after almost three full years of extensive planning, we opened with some 250 students combined, at both schools. The population at the Spanish school was lower, much to our surprise, but undoubtedly due to the fact that the school was located in a less desirable neighborhood. Ascher (1985) pointed out that 'research supports the common view that the distance students travel to a magnet, the attractiveness of the facility, and the safety of the school building and its surroundings all contribute to the magnet school's attractiveness'. The French school was located in a very fine neighborhood, by design, in order to compete directly with a private French school which was successfully operating in the area. We did attract a fair number of these students—and one teacher for the Spanish school, as well.

While racial balance is a factor for the lottery selection of students in all alternative programs in our district, both schools were racially out of balance in the first year of operation as we simply tried to take all students who were interested in attending an immersion school. A closer look indicated that, to a degree, neighborhood populations had opted to attend one of the immersion schools. With the French school in a predominantly white neighborhood and the Spanish school in a predominantly black neighborhood, there were characteristics we had not manipulated to plan for a better racial mix (Rossell in Ascher, 1985). Some teachers at the Spanish school relayed that parents, in fact, had no understanding that the school was a Spanish immersion school in which content was taught in Spanish. For the most part, however, students were there by their parents' choice, some students having parents or grandparents whose native language was French or Spanish.

Parent orientation meetings were held just prior to the opening of school to go over important information in the parent guides. Every effort was made to make parents feel comfortable and secure. The most supportive and vocal parents were tremendously helpful in this area. Parent volunteers offered generously of their time and talents. Rooms were readied; bulletin boards created. Routine matters, such as making sure children knew which bus to ride by providing them with color-coded bus tags, were creatively handled. The staff had to anticipate every single matter which could possibly come up, as well as some way to deal with the matter from the very first moment using a language which was not the child's own. School menus, forms, schedules and other routine items had been created in French and Spanish during the summer and posted in the schools in order to create a total immersion climate there.

Challenges of the first year of operation were not entirely unanticipated. Meetings were scheduled once monthly with the two immersion principals in which we discussed progress and problems and worked at solutions. Many problems were of a nature which was not critical to the educational program, i.e. we wanted the school signs, on the outside of each building, to be in French and in Spanish, to truly represent what one would find on the inside. We also worked toward having professional signs made for the building interior in French or in Spanish, too, to maintain the total atmosphere of the schools. Others were more serious problems which could impede the educational program; i.e. being unable to purchase texts from Canada or France because they required advance payment (not permitted by our district) or because payment would be delayed and incorrect due to the difference in currency. A purchase order, for example, rarely reflected the exact price of materials from another country in spite of calls to a bank to get that day's rate of exchange and so noting the price in American dollars on the purchase order. The lapse in time almost always made exchange rates invalid, not to mention bank fees assessed for conversion of currency; in addition, the shipping expenses were often other than anticipated and at times, there were additional charges for customs. We worked to develop creative solutions but were often caught in bureaucratic webs which were not of our doing.

There was a concerted effort, from the beginning, to keep the two schools as equal as possible, which was not to be a realistic expectation. From the beginning, decisions which were made elsewhere, such as school location, had a great impact on similarities, or lack thereof, within the two schools. Student enrollment and staffing, both already mentioned, caused different amounts and kinds of attention directed to each school. There was a perception, too, of partiality to the French school because they simply had more complex situations which required more extensive consideration and diligence.

Also, almost immediately, it was apparent that the two schools had different 'personalities'. Theoretically, this could have been due to the influence and leadership style of the individual principals. It was most noticeable, however, in the interaction between the students and teachers. Without exception, every teacher in the Spanish school had attended college and received teacher training in the United States. They may have been better equipped to deal with American students. They may have been exposed to more techniques which emphasize positive recognition and feedback for students. They had, in fact, spent more time in American classrooms and knew what to expect. Another observation was that the stereotypical Latin personality allowed frequent use of terms of endearment toward the children ('Amorcito', etc.) while the European-trained teachers in the French school reflected a more distant attitude with the children: if school was the children's job or duty, why should they be rewarded or encouraged for doing what they were supposed to do, expected to do?

Unfortunately, we had not prepared any broad inservice plans; it was as though we all needed a break. We had worked almost non-stop at a grueling and stressful pace. Also, the teachers simply had to 'jump in and do it', learning as they went. They were most likely as prepared as they could have been, under the circumstances. We already feared the reputed burn-out that immersion teachers experience largely because of their heavy workload and hesitated to add one more burden to the teachers' schedules. Also, those teachers who had a temporary teaching certificate were required to enroll in a college or university to earn six semester hours toward their certificate area within the next nine months in order to have their certificate renewed.

Fortunately for us, the local university in which the teachers enrolled provided them with practical classes and experiences which would ultimately help them become better teachers. The first spring, for example, we were permitted to design a course of our own, taught at one of the schools, and with a professor of our own suggestion who would help the immersion teachers define what difficulties they were encountering, and would help them discover solutions and strategies which they would, in turn, share with other members in the class.

In our district, we have a mentor teacher or peer evaluation system in place, PAR (Peer Assistance Review). As spelled out in an agreement with the teachers' union, each teacher in a first-year contract with the public schools is to be assigned a PAR consultant. All but two immersion teachers were in this category. PAR consultants are regarded as master teachers: well-trained, skilled practitioners with an extensive background in sound educational practices. Regular supervision of new teachers, then, could largely be the responsibility of the building principal and PAR consultant.

In theory, this should have relieved some of the pressure on the building principal and the foreign language supervisor; it should also have been a manner to provide a more objective and less emotional response to an individual teacher. What resulted, however, was another obstacle which caused some unfortunate misunderstandings and additional tension. If we had difficulty in finding teachers to staff these schools, where would we find master teachers who thoroughly understood immersion and could help the new teachers in these immersion programs? To assign an elementary-trained PAR consultant was only partially effective. While they could demonstrate expertise in elementary school practices, generally, consultants were intimidated by their lack of knowledge of French or Spanish. To assign a secondary teacher with a thorough knowledge of French or Spanish did not provide a credible avenue of support; these persons knew little or nothing about the elementary classroom and how, on a daily basis, integrated lessons were planned, scheduled and carried out. Through no fault of the PAR program or consultants, not one consultant had a firm enough background in second language acquisition theory and practice to grapple with many of the problems that immersion teachers consistently faced. It was necessary, then, to train the assigned PAR consultants in a crash course on immersion, a task that, given the time and energy necessary, was impossible.

The PAR consultants, however, did serve a valuable role in helping teachers with routine procedures, classroom management and more effective student discipline and in providing them with support and feedback. As with any new teachers, immersion teachers needed help with what was expected of them, and needed to learn such mundane tasks as how to set up a grade book, how to manage paperwork, how to use volunteers effectively. This was coupled with additional routine elementary school procedures they would need to accomplish on a daily basis such as lunchroom counts and lunch money collection and accounting. Principals met with the teachers initially to get them started, but PAR consultants did turn out to be of value in this arena. Also, the PAR program allowed us to arrange cross-visits for our immersion teachers to other elementary classrooms. Spanish and French immersion teachers could visit one another's classrooms as well as monolingual classrooms of exemplary teachers to observe, discuss common problems, and share ideas.

Under the PAR Program, new teachers were evaluated by both the PAR consultant and the building principal. Teachers who were not in their first year of contract with our district, but who were due for an evaluation, were to be evaluated solely by the building principal. While evaluation is not tied to subject area supervisors in the public schools, supervisors are routinely called in for supervision purposes and are often asked to provide input in teacher evaluations. While time-consuming, it was relatively easy to spend large amounts of time in the immersion classrooms, often accompanying the many visitors who requested personal observations of the program. At the request of the principal or the PAR consultant, I made visits and provided feedback and suggestions to teachers.

In spite of the many problems that seemed, at times, insurmountable, the immersion schools were clearly successful in their first year. Parent support and enthusiasm were phenomenal. We scheduled a number of special programs which included open houses, building rededication, young authors programs, holiday assemblies and other opportunities that allowed us to have parents and the general public share in the schools. The schools were featured in several newspaper articles and television news shows. Reactions were always positive, yet the biggest test—how students would perform—was still to come.

From the teachers' point of view, the program seemed to be progressing in the way we had expected; when we wrote program descriptions, decided on percentages and divided subjects, we attempted to make realistic decisions which could be attained. As it turned out, goals were on the conservative side as teachers constantly reported being able to accomplish much more than they had thought they would and were able to go beyond percentage expectations.

From a supervisory point of view, there were still many functions to perform. I served, at times, as a liaison between the schools and other departments in the district. As such, other content supervisors were asked to present workshops for the two staffs. Science, math, reading and writing workshops were held, with attention paid to strategies to accomplish district goals and objectives within an immersion setting. When a problem arose, the two principals would work to solve the problem; they generally notified me and asked for input when appropriate.

The schools were visited by large numbers of people—from the general public, to parents, to potential parents, to high school and university students, to persons from other school districts, to teachers within our own district. Because so many of the secondary foreign language teachers lacked understanding of total immersion, there was a concerted effort to arrange visits for them. Many took advantage of released time to do so; this was extremely effective. Not only did it provide an opportunity for professional growth for them in showing just how immersion worked, it spurred interest in second language acquisition theory and practice and how content-based instruction could also be extended to secondary foreign language classes. Secondary teachers had shared in the benefit of some of the pre-service workshops. The visits provided a natural bridge to the workshop presentations and their classrooms; in addition, the process aided articulation and thinking about future planning for follow-up programs and gave the district an entire cadre of immersion advocates who were eager to promote total immersion in the public schools. We had developed a process for visits since we received so many requests. Generally, the public was encouraged to visit on Tuesday, Wednesday or Thursday. Visitors were identified with special visitor buttons in the target language, and each classroom had special chairs identified as visitor chairs. We also had developed a packet of information and guidelines for visitors and asked each visitor to respond, in writing, following the visit.

Program Maintenance and Support

The summer following the first year of operation was relatively uneventful, except for the legal issues which were not resolved, again, until the last minute. We had some groups working on curriculum planning and development; we had some inservice including a formal sharing session scheduled just prior to the opening of school. We were not equipped to deal with pre-service training for the new hires, except on a rather sporadic basis. The PAR consultants helped to a degree, but generally with non-immersion issues as mentioned earlier in this chapter.

The schools continued to grow in terms of student population, and with great attention at lottery time, became racially balanced, a balance which has been carefully maintained. Media coverage continued to be positive. Student performances, professional conference presentations, speaking engagements and publications stimulated interest in the schools and brought positive recognition to the district. The two principals were selected, by the State language association, as the 1989 recipients of the 'Educator Friend of Foreign Language' Award for their support and dedication to the two immersion schools. In 1990, the immersion programs were recognized by the National Association of School Boards as a winning curricular idea, with descriptions published nationally in *The Learning Bank*.[1] Requests have come in from virtually all over the US for information on our total immersion program.

Recruitment of teachers for the French program continues to be a top priority, but one which has still not met with resolution. In April of 1989, three administrators involved with the French immersion program were sent on a general district recruiting trip to upper New York state. The trip yielded absolutely nothing for either immersion school; however, we did manage to make time to visit a few Canadian universities to talk about their teacher training programs and a possible recruitment plan for the following winter. Attracting Canadian teachers seemed unlikely: a strong job market exists in Canada for immersion teachers with the many programs there (Majhanovich & Fish, 1988) and Canadian teaching salaries are much more attractive than American teaching salaries. Also, our district remained strongly opposed to hiring teachers who would require legal assistance with teaching certificates or visas. While frequent media attention brings, on occasion, local interest from potential candidates, the question of qualified candidates for the French school is undoubtedly our greatest challenge.

In spite of developing a recruiting plan for staff for the French school, including advertising copy in French and a list of newspapers and other publications in which to advertise, with costs for advertising, there was no response initially from the personnel department other than, as mentioned, a firm resolve not to hire anyone needing a visa. The second summer, we were permitted to place ads in various newspapers in Louisiana. The timing was much too late; we got no response. Finally, three years into the program, advertisements were placed in Canadian newspapers in a timely manner. Unfortunately, the bureaucracy of a large district prevented teacher allocations from being approved quickly enough which left us with a surprisingly strong field of Canadian candidates to whom we could not make any definite offers, and for whom we would need more time than we had available to solve visa and certification questions. In the meantime, legal questions for teachers we already have on board have continued to be unsettled with each progressive year. The legalities can often prevent foreign nationals from traveling back to their homeland, which, in turn, can cause further stress and frustration for them.

The series of challenges of the ensuing years, which, realistically, we knew we would face and may very well always face were confirmed by our visits to other districts; the greatest struggles are with human and material resources, well-articulated follow-up programs, and administrative support. Among the three aspects of administrative support required for successful magnet programs (McMillan, 1980) is openness of communication, the lack of which is directly related to our problems with human resources (already discussed) and follow-up programs.

Articulated sequences and follow-through programs all the way through high school had been a topic for investigation and recommendations well before the elementary immersion schools had even opened their doors. Immersion follow-through had been planned for the 1989–90 school year, when we would actually have students who had immersion experience moving to grade six. Students from the first and second years of the program who would be leaving the fifth grade would not really have experienced immersion before that time. As noted earlier, the plan developed by the two elementary staffs had called for overt language teaching, rather than content teaching through the language, in grades four and five for the first two years of operation. That left, in theory, two full years to prepare for a middle school immersion program which should have been adequate.

Early indications were that we could have guaranteed seats for these students in the foreign language/international studies middle school so that they could continue, in grade six, with foreign language classes and eventually, immersion classes. When the time came for the actual commitment, we lacked the administrative support to make this happen. It left many people terribly upset; it also convinced us that changing personnel in the upper levels of administration undermined the support we had previously counted upon. There was no way to anticipate how an initiative to totally reform the district just two years after their implementation would affect the immersion schools; a national phenomenon of urban districts' difficulty in attracting and holding a superintendent for any length of time leaves the future uncertain. Due to the frequent turn-over of superintendents and ensuing lack of stability, there seems to be a fair amount of upheaval in upper administrative ranks. As new personnel come and the move continues toward site-based management, there seems to have been reason to appoint new committees to report on these same topics over and over again.

The question of program continuation still needs a definite resolution. Plans have been developed on any number of occasions. We have already established a grade six and a grade seven immersion continuation program at the foreign language/international studies middle school. The program at grade eight is already well-defined, too, and ready to be added with the next school year. Each year, however, the issue of guaranteed seat allotments at the middle school must be revisited. Staffing continues to be our greatest problem as we search for candidates who are appropriate for middle schoolers, have elementary or specific subject certification, are informed about or interested in immersion teaching and second language acquisition, and are native or near native in language ability and cultural experience.

We continue to scour conferences and communicate with other districts for appropriate materials to purchase as we further develop the program. The issue of material resources seems to have stabilized. With more FLES programs being developed, we see more materials of high quality that are available to us. Bilingual programs in Spanish have spurred textbook companies to produce quality products. Diligent searches for quality materials in Canada and relationships developed there have benefitted the French school.

In terms of assessing the success of the schools, we had nothing formal in place as the schools opened. After four years of operation, we can point at the fact that enrollment continues to grow at both schools. Parent satisfaction is quite evident; we continue to receive positive reaction from the many visitors we have. Various ethnic groups in the community, particularly Hispanic ones, reach out to establish ties with the schools.

Formal evaluation of student progress has been in place. District wide testing, for example, does occur and is now mandated by state law. The tests are given in English. As noted earlier in this chapter, results have indicated that students would perform as well as, or better than, their peers in monolingual schools, which occurs in spite of the fact that students are taught in the second language but are tested in English. With great attention to the development of our total immersion schools based upon the successes of other US immersion schools we had visited, we were confident that our schools would produce similar results. In fact, our test results continue to be very impressive. Students in both schools score above the district-wide averages in all areas tested and have placed among the top five in the district, within 86 elementary schools, in several content areas in successive years. The need exists, however, to publish and disseminate a thorough study of these test results by our immersion students.

Future Immersion Considerations

If immersion programs are to continue to grow and succeed, there must be substantial attention to future considerations for elementary foreign language instruction. These include advocacy, teacher training, resources (financial, material, human), expanded opportunities for early language learning, articulation, research and evaluation (Met & Rhodes, 1990).

In terms of advocacy, immersion school administrators have a responsibility to promote the importance of language learning in the elementary school. While noting that immersion is not for everyone, these administrators should be conversant on the various models and program goals and expectations and be able to speak to reasons for implementing and maintaining immersion. They must continue to seek support among district and government decision makers, parents, community and other foreign language professionals.

Teacher training is an area of vital interest, as outlined in various sections of this book. Work has been accomplished in Canadian universities which outline areas in which immersion teachers should receive training. The 1986 Frisson-Rickson and Rebuffot study delineates a proposal for the training and retraining of immersion teachers.[2] The proposed program is very thorough and may require five years to accomplish all aspects. The Bernhardt and Schrier study (this volume) may serve as a basis for immersion teacher training in the US.

Financial resources may not be as critical a problem as some others, since, in theory, immersion programs do not add additional expense to elementary classrooms. The cost-effectiveness, success and parent support of immersion programs should ensure their continuation in spite of district cutbacks. Expenses involving legal matters and additional costs for importing books and materials or for curriculum development are factors that create financial hardships for immersion schools and those which require a commitment for continued support.

Material resources, as noted earlier, are becoming easier to find. There is still a need for local schools to develop curricular materials for topics that are distinctive to their district or area (i.e. state or city history). That is, it is often difficult to find materials that are both age and language appropriate and that reflect the adopted course of study for a particular grade.

Human resources have been a recurring theme all through this chapter. If immersion programs are to grow, then attention needs to be given to developing effective teacher training programs to establish a supply of qualified candidates. If a district must rely on foreign nationals, legal requirements need to be addressed. As districts will find, visas may be renewed only for a specified number of years, depending on visa type, and only on a yearly basis. New requests must be filed annually with no guarantee that the visas will be renewed. Well in advance of the final year of eligibility for renewal, some policy has to be established for permanent residency visas. If the district decides to help foreign teachers seek permanent residency status, the question of who will pay the legal fees will arise. Our district settled on a compromise in which the legal fees were split between the candidate and the district. Any school district in this situation will also learn that simply aiding a candidate, mainly by agreeing that employment will be available for that candidate, will not guarantee that the candidate must continue working for the district. After paying legal fees and honoring employment offers, a district may find that the candidate who gained permanent residency status could choose to work elsewhere.

The leadership for such specialized schools can make or break a program. As a future direction for foreign language professionals, we need to work on the nurturing of principals at all levels who will administer and advocate foreign language schools in an authoritative, informed manner. For that matter, it is my own personal conviction that foreign language educators are too insular and need to seek out other positions of authority in educational institutions where they can make a difference through influence, decision-making and policy development. Building and central office administration positions rarely attract foreign language educators; it is precisely from these positions that critical decisions are made which most greatly impact foreign language programs.

Articulation has also been a recurring theme in this chapter. One of the major aims of early language learning is to provide language study in a long, well-articulated sequence. Met & Rhodes (1990) note that 'well articulated programs are a result of consensus, careful planning and monitoring among language teachers, administrators and concerned parents across levels'. Foreign language supervisors are well aware, too, of the political realities that can sometimes obliterate the consensus, careful planning, and monitoring within immersion programs. My personal concern for this city's immersion programs lies most heavily within the topic of well-articulated follow-up programs. The leadership within these schools, both parents and administrators, have an obligation to continue working toward district commitment to solve articulation problems.

Conclusion

Trying to make any public school system function effectively in today's world is a difficult task. Trying to provide equity in educational opportunities and to be simultaneously responsive to individual community members' needs as well as neighborhood concerns is a full time challenge. As Salomone (this volume) rightly points out, immersion is indeed a 'double challenge'. While Salomone wrote those words referring to teachers, the descriptor is also more than appropriate for supervisors of such programs. My task as a supervisor was to facilitate the implementation of a new elementary magnet program. But that implementation task became all the more intense because there were unique materials, personnel, legal, and cultural issues involved.

Glenwood and Greystone may or may not be textbook cases for coursework toward Supervisory certification. My hope is that my perspectives here lend advice and support to supervisors charged with similar challenges. But most importantly, I want to communicate that such challenges are indeed worth the time and commitment they demand.

Notes to Chapter 7

1. *The Learning Bank*, August 1990, c/o *The American School Board Journal*, 1680 Duke Street, Alexandria, VA 22314, USA. Tel: (703) 838-6722.
2. *The Training and Retraining of Immersion Teachers: Towards Establishing National Standards*, by Francine Frisson-Rickson and Jacques Rebuffot, is available through the Canadian Association of Immersion Teachers and is also discussed in the article by Majhanovich and Fish.

8 Immersion: A Principal's Perspective

ROGER COFFMAN

Introduction

Any examination of a school's educational program should include the building principal's perspective. Much has been said about the key role played by the building principal in the overall effectiveness of a school's program. This role seems to take on new meaning for the language immersion school principal. Being principal of an immersion school is much the same as being principal in a conventional school. Yet, there are some genuine differences as well as some not-so-obvious differences. To say that the job description of the language immersion school principal is much more complex than that of a regular school principal is a significant understatement.

What follows is my perspective as principal of an elementary immersion school in a large, midwestern, urban school district. An historical background on planning and development during the initial five years is followed by a discussion of issues involving the establishment of a language immersion program. There is also an attempt throughout to reflect on the relevance of the 'knowledges' that one acquires which are important in administering a language immersion program within the total school setting. It is assumed that the underlying consideration or motivational force is the children we serve, and that all of our efforts should ultimately focus on meeting their educational needs. With all due respect to the many professional colleagues in other school districts both in the US and other countries who have had a great impact on the development of our program, there is no intent to compare or imply a definitive word of authority. The intent is to share and hopefully, enlighten.

Historical Background

Glenwood Immersion School is a K-5 alternative (magnet) school, opened in the fall of 1987, in a previously-closed building. (For a more complete historical portrait, see Ging, this volume). Located on a spacious, well-landscaped lot in a residential area in the northwestern part of the city, the one-storey physical plant contains 14 classrooms, a gymnasium/lunchroom, library learning center, and office complex.

Currently Glenwood has a full student capacity, with two self-contained classes of 25 students each at each grade level, K-5, and a total of 300 students (48% black, 52% non-black). There are eleven classroom teachers as well as nine full-time support staff members and numerous parent volunteers. Supplemental instruction (in English) is provided for second grade reading, science, art, vocal music, instrumental music, and physical education. There is a library learning center, containing materials in both the immersion language and in English, a microcomputer lab and computers in each classroom. Students are bussed from all areas of the city.

Being Principal

Although the principal plays a crucial role in the successful implementation of any school's educational program, the immersion school principal's role is even more vital, requiring additional talents, skills, and qualifications. As pressures grow for change and reform in our schools, to meet the changing and expanding needs of our students, the building principal, as administrator and instructional leader, will continue to be the key player at the building level—the person who helps establish a school climate unique to each school's personality and conducive to fostering positive teaching and learning. That 'key player' must first be an advocate for children, as well as supporter of teachers, cheerleader, motivator, enabler, facilitator, organizer, ensurer of student safety and self, and positive 'people person'. The ideal principal should possess the unlimited knowledge, wisdom, patience, energy, people skills, and positive attitude needed to make a successful school. Specialized graduate-level university training as well as teaching and education-related experiences are also important qualifications.

Generally, expectations for the immersion school are the same as those for the conventional schools: (e.g. creating a positive learning climate, following the prescribed local curriculum, meeting district-wide obligations and expectations, meeting the individual educational needs of every child, participating in school activities and celebrations, and maintaining high test scores on standardized, norm-referenced tests in math and English language arts and reading). But there are also the expectations of the immersion program itself. Hence, the immersion principal must possess the expected characteristics of a 'good principal' as well as be instructional leader for a unique curricular and teaching setting that takes place in another language.

The question naturally arises about whether it is important for the principal to be fluent in the school's particular immersion language. It is definitely important for the principal to have a working knowledge of the language. Clearly, finding a person with all of the other necessary prerequisites for effective 'principalling' who also has a functional fluency equal to that of the classroom teacher's is rare. Personally, I have found that my interest in and study of the immersion language, as well as foreign languages in general, have enabled me to be an equal, knowledgeable participant in the on-going development of the program. Though not completely fluent, I know what is going on in the classrooms and in staff meetings and understand the learning and teaching processes experienced by students and teachers. Study and frequent travel, an extensive background in teaching and language arts/reading/writing, and prior administrative experience have helped me feel prepared.

Nevertheless, there are many times when I have felt overwhelmed, frustrated, and inadequate, to the point of asking myself, 'What have I gotten myself into?' At the very least, the immersion principal must be knowledgeable about the school's immersion goals, well-versed in current research and theory regarding first- and second-language acquisition and immersion instruction, able to relate to what the classroom teacher is experiencing and doing with students, and have a strong interest in the immersion program and the language of instruction. The principal, as the immersion school's main advocate, must be well-prepared to assume this challenging role.

Planning to open

Obviously, thorough prior research and planning are necessary before attempting to initiate a language immersion program. Perhaps it is impossible to begin planning too soon, though in reality we are rarely given as much lead time as we would like when undertaking such a project. As soon as building principals were appointed in February, 1987, we began preparations for the August, 1987, opening. At the same time, we were continuing to serve as principals of other buildings for the remainder of that school year. I mention this because it is a good example of a typical extra challenge: budget constraints do not always allow for ideal conditions, and the potential immersion principal needs to be aware of this.

Initially, it is important for those charged with initial planning to understand exactly what immersion is, and what an immersion school looks and feels like. Accordingly, we reviewed important immersion research and descriptive articles (Met, 1987; Curtain & Pesola, 1988; Andrade & Ging, 1988; Swain, 1982), and visited several noted successful American immersion schools. Those visits and numerous subsequent return visits by myself and teachers as well proved to be invaluable and well worth the time and expense involved.

Regardless of whether or not one feels prepared for a task, time constraints will usually dictate the need to translate ideas into a tangible action plan. After drafting general goals and ideas about what an immersion program should 'look like', we set about identifying the specifics needed to get a new instructional program underway. Initial program planning and development for two immersion programs was done together. But since every school environment is unique, with its own 'personality' and set of circumstances, much of the actual program implementation is the responsibility of the principal and staff, with support from the foreign language supervisor, other district personnel, parents, and community leaders. For Glenwood the circumstances were: re-opening a previously closed building and implementing a magnet school immersion program at the same time.

The tasks related to re-opening the closed building were somewhat routine, if involved. The physical plant was readied through repairing, cleaning, landscaping, and painting; rooms were furnished; general school supplies, books, paper, etc. were ordered; support personnel was selected; system-wide procedures were implemented. The school was prepared to receive students and teachers in late August.

Concurrently, there were many identified tasks and areas for discussion and decision making related to getting the immersion program underway. Among the most important were: establishing an effective school learning climate; selecting a competent, qualified teaching staff; defining and building the instructional program; procuring and developing instructional materials; providing initial and on-going staff development opportunities; and recruiting students for the program. Of course, most of these issues are interconnected and are not dealt with in isolation. Also, it is not merely a matter of handling them and sweeping them aside, or assuming that the principal will autonomously handle them. Much cooperation is required. As additional affected parties such as staff and parents come on board, they, too must be involved in the overall decision- making and execution processes. These six important areas are discussed in further detail below.

School Climate

Many factors help create a school's distinct personality and effective learning environment. The building principal plays a major role in helping to establish that school climate. Early attention to these factors helps set the tone and initiate a positive outlook. In Glenwood's case, the task was a bit more all-encompassing, (and perhaps more advantageous) since it involved both a school-opening and program implementation. There was a conscious decision made that Glenwood be a fairly typical, conventional elementary school; the difference would be in its instructional program. Attention was thus given to the conventional questions about building organization, student management and motivation, and building positive attitudes in staff, all of which encourage a positive, receptive atmosphere. But additional attention was given to extra details that would reinforce the school's cultural flavor—e.g. ensuring that all signs and displays in hallways and common areas have text in the second language (L2) only, placing L2 posters and artwork in the office, displaying the school's name in the second language on the outside of the building, identifying all teachers and classrooms with signs in L2, encouraging culturally and linguistically appropriate visuals on classroom bulletin boards, prominently displaying flags of L2 speaking countries in the hallways—visual touches that have a definite initial impact to anyone entering the building. Other details included answering the telephone with a second language greeting and including a few, recognizable L2 words in correspondence to parents. Though some of these might at first thought appear to be rather superficial, they do have a positive impact and help create that special flavor.

Staffing

Finding competent, qualified classroom immersion teachers is, no doubt, the single most important and difficult challenge in building an effective language immersion program. This has been especially emphasized by our colleagues at other immersion schools who also continue to wrestle with this issue. While other factors are certainly important, the most important factors contributing to the success of any instructional program are the teacher and the masterful interaction and impact that each teacher has on each student. This is no less important for the immersion instructional program.

What are the desired ideal characteristics of an elementary language immersion teacher? They are the same as for any elementary classroom teacher coupled with the challenge of teaching in a language non- native to the students. The teacher should be a child-centered, energetic, competent, qualified individual who can be certified to teach as a regular elementary classroom teacher. In addition, the teacher must be knowledgeable about curriculum and instruction, especially as they relate to the teaching of elementary reading and language arts, and must understand how to manage, motivate, and instruct elementary age youngsters. It is also most desirable for the candidate to be knowledgeable about second language acquisition and current research related to studies of immersion teaching and to have had successful experience teaching in an immersion classroom. I have yet to be convinced that a separate, special university teacher preparatory program or separate teacher certification requirements are necessary or desirable. I am most concerned about finding a 'good' elementary teacher. However, the single qualification absolutely essential and not negotiable is having native or near-native fluency in the immersion language. This term 'fluency' tends to be interpreted in many ways. I regard the required 'classroom-functional' fluency as that which is characterized by such ease and command of usage (speaking, reading, writing, and understanding) of the language that it presents no barrier or hindrance to the normal classroom teaching-learning process. Moreover, it is so spontaneous and automatic as to enable the teacher to maintain a natural, child-centered classroom environment, filled with rich language experiences based on the individual needs of students and the content and skills to be taught. Language competence should be assumed, separate from all of the other teaching qualifications.

The issue of determining a non-native-speaking candidate's language fluency and all candidates' suitability for teaching in the immersion classroom has posed problems with those persons traditionally responsible for the recruitment and hiring of teachers. These district personnel directors and teacher recruiters often lack knowledge of the language and/or of understanding the teaching needs of the immersion program. Often, building principals are not allowed input into the recruiting or hiring of teachers. This is a major concern.

Fortunately, we have been able to work in collaboration with our district personnel directors, who have relied on us for advice, guidance, and professional judgement. As a result, the personnel department, principal, staff, and foreign language supervisor have all been involved in the teacher recruitment and selection process, especially as it relates to language competence, fluency, and suitability for immersion teaching. We used a procedure whereby a potential candidate is invited for an interview by a team of interviewers at the building level. The team consists of three or four persons—the principal, two or three classroom teachers (one native speaker, if possible), and perhaps the foreign language supervisor or a second-language fluent university professor. Questions relate to general teaching issues, immersion familiarity, and student management/motivation. At least part of the interview is done in the immersion language. There is a strong attempt to make the process as relaxed and non-threatening as possible.

We have found that after participating in over 100 such interviews, it is possible to make fairly accurate group decisions about the potential suitability of a perspective applicant. However, it is most difficult to quantify the desired qualities, especially as they relate to language fluency, since the actual 'mix' of desired qualities and qualifications for each candidate can be so different and yet still so suitable. It has been suggested that we use the ACTFL Oral Proficiency Rating Scale 'superior' rating as the minimum acceptable rating; however, I am not convinced that this truly 'gets at' the heart of what we are looking for and can only be considered a means for being 'in the ballpark'.

Once Glenwood's actual teacher needs were identified in February, 1987, the personnel department, foreign language supervisor and I located eight prospective teacher candidates. In tandem with 15 other newly-developing magnet school programs, a process was set up for posting the positions locally and assigning building interview teams to interview candidates. We were able to select three excellent local candidates—two Americans and one native speaker currently living in our city. What we discovered (and continue to find) is that most American candidates are elementary-certified teachers who have studied some foreign language in high school or college, high school foreign language teachers who are familiar with teaching the language but who may or may not possess the needed fluency, fluent L2 candidates with no teacher training or experience in public schools, or foreign candidates who have experience teaching the L2 in their own country but who may or may not be L2 fluent. None of these candidates were quite suitable. We still receive many applications from interested candidates who are not fluent in the immersion language, do not have an elementary teaching certificate (or possibly any teacher certificate), are not familiar with American kids or curriculum, and/or do not have visas or work permits. After exhaustive searches for candidates in the US through job postings, newspaper advertisements and contacts with university placement offices in key areas of the country, we decided to consider foreign teacher candidates. After several months of searching, more fully described in Ging (this volume), five suitable foreign teachers were hired to teach at Glenwood.

The hiring of foreign candidates can pose some serious issues which need to be considered. Aside from the cultural differences, (also an advantage), a lack of familiarity with American children and curriculum can lead to misunderstandings and problems in classroom management. Teaching methods in other countries are often different; teacher-training programs, while thorough, may be part of a completely different system, which leads to difficulties in equating and evaluating the training in American terms. This in turn can lead to difficulties in obtaining proper teacher certification from state departments of education. And of course, obtaining visas is always a costly, complicated, and time-consuming venture. However, the foreign-born teachers have proven to be a great asset and add much to the richness of our program. Their teacher preparation appears to be at least equal to that of most US trained teachers; they are intelligent, creative, knowledgeable, high-energy teachers who are a valued part of our staff.

It is important to include a few words about the support staff. The term 'school staff' implies all members of the staff—the secretary, custodians, educational aides, food service workers, and special teachers, as well as classroom teachers. These staff members are vital to the overall smooth operation of a school. I am especially dependent on our hard-working secretary and head custodian! However, for reasons often not in the principal's control, these important people often do not speak or understand the school's immersion language. This can create problems because there is a desire to use the language as much as possible throughout the building. People can feel 'left out' and not a part of the staff. It is wise to address this issue and find a solution that fits the particular building program's needs; nevertheless, the support and team-work of the entire staff is an important consideration. The staffing issue in language immersion schools is complex and time-consuming, yet crucial to the over-all success of the immersion program. (The amount of importance I place on it is obvious from the amount of space I devote to it now!) There are many things to consider, and many trade-offs, regardless of how the program is staffed. We have been fortunate at Glenwood to have been supported by a school district administration and personnel department which recognizes our need for special considerations, efforts, and expenses necessary for finding qualified, effective teachers.

Instructional Program

Defining and building the immersion instructional program should be the major focus of a school's efforts and attention. Usually, an individual school is operating with some basic instructional 'givens' like a system-wide prescribed course of study for each subject area and grade level, for example. When instituting a new program, such as language immersion, it is important to first consider the basic assumptions or ground rules, and then to formulate a program philosophy, general program goals, and specific program objectives, along with strategies or processes for achieving those goals and objectives.

We spent a lot of time with our staff and with the other immersion school staff as well, building working relationships and learning as much as possible about language immersion. This enabled us to identify and clarify our own basic ideas about immersion, define and describe the total elementary language immersion programs for our schools, and then formulate program philosophy, goals and instructional strategies. This type of program planning process is fluid, evolving and on-going; it requires continual interaction and planning both at the building level and in conjunction with the other immersion school staff, as well. The overall goal should continue to provide an effective instructional program that fits the immersion program instructional goals and meets the instructional needs of our children.

Materials

Having on hand a wide array of appropriate instructional materials is another important component of an effective instructional program. Immersion teachers need to rely especially on such items as visuals, manipulatives, big books, cassettes, and video tapes, as well as textbooks and story books. Teachers must be allowed the time to help make decisions about locating, selecting, buying, organizing, cataloging, storing, and effectively using materials. Some foreign language materials for elementary-age students are not readily available in the US and require extra efforts and expense to procure. It goes without saying that many foreign language materials need to be created, modified, or translated to fit a particular school's curriculum, especially in content areas unique to American culture. Time must be provided for teachers to develop these materials. As a program continues to expand and evolve, and as program needs continue to change, there is an on-going need to locate or develop appropriate materials.

We have particularly concentrated on making our library a true learning and resource center. Since the building originally contained no library, we were able to design one to suit our specific needs. We investigated the varying ways that other immersion schools choose to house their foreign language library collections. We chose to create two separate, adjoining spaces for our bilingual materials, with separate filing and cataloging. Each classroom is scheduled into the LLC twice each week, once for an English language experience and book selection—and once for the same in the foreign language. We have tried to maintain the two separate experiences, even for the younger, total immersion students, to encourage parents to read to their children at home.

We are fortunate to have a very talented, hardworking library aide who not only assists students when they come to the library and orders materials, but who also has organized materials, compiled computerized lists of our L2 materials, and implemented a computerized check-out system for all books. Currently, we have over 3500 foreign language titles, in addition to our other L2 and English materials. We have also been fortunate to have the support of our field librarian from the district's central library department, which has given us an unusual amount of building autonomy and latitude in selecting, ordering, and processing our own materials at the local building level.

Staff Development

The need for staff development activities is another on-going concern that relates to and helps fulfill the previously mentioned needs: creating the school learning climate, selecting staff, designing an instructional program, and selecting and developing materials. Glenwood's initial pre-opening needs were best met through a series of sessions attended by both language immersion school staffs. There was specific time allotted to interaction, information-gathering, goal setting, and program planning. Noted experts in the field of immersion were invited to lead sessions; in addition there were times when our group met separately. The usefulness of these initial meetings cannot be overemphasized.

At the building level, on-going program concerns have been addressed through countless meetings and presentations as well as arranged visits to other immersion schools. As new teachers are hired each year, they must be given added opportunities to learn about immersion instruction. There are also system needs and expectations that require our staff's participation: competency-based education, career education, microcomputer instruction, and multicultural concerns. We also found it useful to continue meetings with both immersion school staffs to deal with common instructional issues.

Dealing with foreign teachers has required attention to other kinds of concerns. Because of a lack of relative familiarity with American students and with issues concerning positive student motivation and management, we have devoted considerable staff development time to these concerns. Teachers have also visited regular elementary classrooms observing teachers in conventional schools. And because their previous university teacher training was not considered entirely parallel or equivalent to the American system, those teachers have also been required to take additional university coursework for teacher certification purposes. A local university has proven to be most understanding and flexible in this regard, allowing us to help tailor the content of courses to meet the teachers' immediate needs at the building level.

It is important to add that the principal also needs to be a part of the staff development process, from the standpoint of learning and growing and also to establish and maintain credibility as the instructional leader of the building. I additionally have tried to make myself better-prepared for carrying out my responsibilities through professional reading, attendance at professional conferences, networking with other immersion educators, visits to other immersion programs, and university coursework, including a five week foreign study program. These professional growth activities have taken considerable extra time, energy, and expense; however, I believe that they have contributed to my overall effectiveness in carrying out my responsibilities as immersion principal.

Additional important issues

There are additional issues related to establishing and maintaining a language immersion program which should not be overlooked. As with the issues previously mentioned, they depend on staff attention and assistance; however, as one might expect the overall, on-going responsibility falls squarely on the principal's shoulders.

'Specialness'

Any unique instructional program that depends on choice should be 'special' and attractive so that students will want to attend. The fact that the program is language immersion, in general, and a specific language in particular, makes it special already. And attention to outward, visual details such as signs in L2, help add to that 'specialness'. But it is still important to design special school-wide activities and events that capitalize on the foreign language instructional emphasis, demonstrate to parents some tangible proof of their child's participation and progress in the program, and build school spirit and pride. At Glenwood, for example, we plan school spirit days and exchanges with classes in other schools; we have pen pals in other language immersion schools; we celebrate special occasions like National Foreign Language Week, Mardi Gras, and St. Nicholas Day; we provide opportunities for students to perform for other students, parents, and the community; we have daily announcements made by students in the L2.

These activities are in addition to the other routine (but important) activities and events such as safety patrol, student council, orchestra, Halloween, etc. We have also chosen a school mascot (Koala), school colors (blue and black) and sold special T-shirts, sweatshirts, mugs, pencils, etc. We recognize student effort and achievement through a monthly 'Exemplary Citizen' program and frequent award assemblies, using L2 text award certificates. The intent is to try to make the school and its program special, a place where learning another language is fun and where students enjoy going to school.

Advertising

A special program that depends on attracting students for its existence needs to advertise. Admittedly, an immersion school in the American midwest creates enough curiosity to attract some media attention. Nevertheless, positive public relations are important and need to be cultivated by the immersion principal. It is important to maintain contact with television and news media, and to invite coverage of important school events. We have assembled collections of slides, produced and created informative videotapes, assembled scrapbooks, and produced pamphlets, flyers, and video displays for student recruiting and for public presentations about Glenwood. Continual attention to advertising is especially important as we compete for students with 21 other elementary magnet schools in the district and continue to build support for our program within the community.

Multicultural Aspects

All schools help children understand and gain an appreciation for diversities as well as similiarities among cultures and ethnic groups in their local, national, and world communities. This importance is underscored in the urban school setting, where student populations are often a rich ethnic and racial mixture. The language immersion program offers a perfect vehicle for exposing students to other cultures, and in so doing, helps them understand and appreciate differences among themselves. At Glenwood we are able to provide this experience in a natural way; as we are challenged to infuse multicultural aspects into our curriculum in an on-going manner, we find that the very nature of our program facilitates the process: emphasis on language and culture; teachers from various countries; and students of various ethnic and racial backgrounds.

It should be noted that with a large population of black students, it is important to be responsive to the special concerns of parents in the black community. Despite considerable effort by the school system, we have been able to find very few qualified black immersion teacher applicants. As a result, we can provide no black teacher role models in the school, which may send mixed signals to black students about the relative significance and importance of another language and culture to them. A further on-going issue is helping all teachers, especially those from Europe, learn how to effectively motivate, manage, and instruct American students from diverse ethnic and cultural backgrounds. This is a very sensitive, important issue, certainly not unique to Glenwood, and yet compounded by Glenwood's individual set of circumstances. Additionally, the school's noncentralized geographic location in a predominantly white neighborhood away from black residential areas requires special additional recruiting efforts to make black parents aware of the school and its program. We continue to focus on these issues, to discuss them, and to find strategies that will help us meet the educational needs of *all* children.

Articulation with Middle School and High School

One of the first questions asked by prospective immersion parents regards what happens to their child upon completion of grade five at Glenwood. Although we know from other immersion programs that not all students choose to continue in an immersion program beyond grade five, an opportunity must be provided for them to do so in order to reinforce and strengthen the foreign language skills already acquired. Research shows the unquestionable need for such reinforcement—without it, students will lose much of what they have gained during the K-5 immersion experience. Concern among Glenwood parents about providing an effective middle school immersion program continues to grow as students progress successfully through the elementary program and need to build and extend their skills. Parents also fear that the lack of a continuation program could jeopardize the growth and value of the elementary program. A developing middle school continuation program is currently offered to students upon completion of grade five. However, further attention must be given to curriculum and staffing. It appears that the provision of a continuation program for middle and high school is a concern of most other immersion programs as well. Such a program will require efforts on the part of all concerned to help 'push' the issue with the ultimate decision makers.

Program Evaluation

A final issue that must be mentioned is evaluation. In this age of increasing accountability, schools are expected to show that their instructional programs are effectively impacting students. Although a variety of evaluation processes are most desirable, this often translates into norm-referenced and criterion-referenced testing of basic skill areas in English. Pressure to improve test scores is mounting, but immersion schools are in a good position to withstand the pressures, due to the proven effectiveness of the instructional program and the proven results regarding the transfer of language skills from the immersion language to English. Glenwood's test scores in math and English reading and language arts have in fact been among the highest of all elementary schools in our district, thus clearly supporting the research.

In the area of measuring students' progress in second language acquisition, various immersion schools rely heavily on establishing local criteria, teacher judgement, and conferencing. Norm-referenced tests in the immersion language that attempt to evaluate student progress in L2 language skills have not been extensively developed. I suspect that there will be additional pressure brought upon immersion programs to prove their worth by producing students' test scores derived from standardized testing instruments. Immersion educators need to give proactive rather than reactive attention to this issue.

Dealing With People

Without question, for me and many of my administrative colleagues, the most important, challenging, time-consuming, frustrating, exciting, and rewarding role of the principal is dealing with people and the situations that arise through human interactions. This human relations aspect is woven through the entire fabric of the job description. The principal must have the skills, sensitivity, patience, and positive attitude to effectively interact with students, motivate and foster working relationships among staff members and deal with parents, members of the community and other education professionals. Once again, for the immersion principal possessing good 'people skills' is essential.

There are some additional immersion-related issues as well. Cultural differences among staff members of different nationalities and backgrounds often lead to differing views, miscommunication and misunderstanding. Lack of a second language background by building support personnel can lead to feelings of separateness and second-class status. The very nature of many persons who choose to work in innovative settings— intelligent, hard-working, independent, adventurous, and creative 'risk-takers'—tends to create the potential for more 'synergy' and the ensuing spin-off resulting from these intense human interactions.

Parental support and involvement is an extraordinarily important component of the successful immersion program, as well. Parents who choose such a program for their children have an additional vested interest in the success of the program. The principal must spend time explaining the program to potential parents, welcoming them into the building, and reassuring them as questions and anxieties arise (i.e. will my child ever learn to read in English?). The principal must also encourage them to volunteer their time at school and encourage active involvement in the school's parent group. We are so fortunate to have had active, visible parent involvement in our school. In such a program as language immersion, with its specialized needs and problems, parents who are closely associated with the program are relied upon to effectively lobby on its behalf with 'higher-ups' in order to get things done.

The unique immersion program attracts many visitors—potential parents, interested foreign language educators, and other curious community members. It is to the school's advantage to encourage such visitors, while ensuring, of course, that their visits do not disturb the learning atmosphere for students and teachers. At Glenwood we have made special provisions for visitors, including a special regular weekly visitation time, a visitor's badge (in the immersion language) and a visitor's informational packet that includes visitation guidelines and a map. This has helped to foster positive impressions and yet allow for minimal disruption to teaching and learning.

This regard for balance of needs was certainly evident during our involvement with the project chronicled in this book. There were both responsibilities and derived benefits for all parties concerned. But since the project's school involvement was occurring at the same time as the usual school routines and teaching responsibilities, there was a constant protective need on my part to facilitate a cooperative balance between normalcy and achievement of project goals, while minimizing disruption and intrusion upon the school, students, and staff.

Participation in the project is also a prime example of the value of networking with the school's various constituencies. Continuous interaction with parents, the community, and other educators within the school system in order to explain the program, build support for it and, at times, defend it is essential. The program must have support and backing in order to sustain itself and grow. It is also important to interact, share, and learn from other immersion programs, and to participate in professional associations. Our visits and contacts with other immersion programs have been valuable. The need to work together to solve common on-going issues is evident. The willingness and cordiality extended by all is appreciated and gratifying.

On-going issues

Most of the initial immersion issues continue to be important issues. From our interaction with other, more experienced immersion programs, we recognize the need to address challenging immersion issues in order to maintain viable language immersion programs.

There are circumstances, often beyond our ability to change or control, that will have an impact on all schools. And there is the constant need for the principal to be a strong advocate for the immersion program. School system priorities change; upper level district superiors, superintendents, and school boards change; and budget constraints due to district funding problems can lead to hard decision-making about program cuts. In addition, growing public demands for greater accountability lead to pressures about increasing test scores. And the growing complexity and range of students' educational needs in today's changing, pluralistic society require greater attention to meeting those needs.

At the school level, there are some concrete, program-related issues that continue to require our attention, i.e. recruitment of students and teachers; materials selection and development; evaluation of students' immersion language skills; deciding at what grade English reading and writing should be introduced; deciding how and when to force or push students to speak the immersion language; deciding when to accept new students into the program; helping non-L2 speaking support staff feel part of the building program; effectively involving parents and volunteers in our school; middle school/high school articulation; and substitute teachers. Some other ongoing program issues are equally important but much more difficult to solve: maintaining students' interest in the program as well as attrition of students (leading to smaller classes and split classes in upper grades); meeting the wide range of student needs and abilities; pre-service and in-service training for teachers; planning time for teachers; teacher 'burn-out'; obtaining visas; and teacher certification for foreign teachers. The list of tasks might seem overwhelming, but through cooperation and hard work the tasks can be effectively addressed.

Conclusion

Looking back over the past five years, I have found that being an immersion principal is much harder than I ever imagined—the principal must deal with many additional program-related issues and be a strong advocate for the program, the school and the students. The principal plays an important role in 'bringing all the ends together'. It has been a professionally gratifying and positive experience. I have attempted to share my own thoughts and feelings about starting a new language immersion school, not as a voice of authority but as a voice of experience and hard work.

As evidenced by the ever-increasing numbers of programs, foreign language immersion has proven to be instructionally effective for students. Building an effective program is a result of the collaborative efforts of many people. At Glenwood we are fortunate to have committed staff members and involved parents. We also have the assistance and solid support of supervising administrators, support personnel and the board of education.

It should not be implied that all is perfect or that we are where we want to be; we continue to work on many challenges and issues with one main goal in mind—providing a quality instructional program that strives to meet the varied educational needs of our students.

Bibliography

ALTWERGER, B., EDELSKY, C. and FLORES, B. 1987, Whole language: What's new? *The Reading Teacher* 41 (2), 144–54.

ANDERSON, L., EVERTSON, C. and BROPHY, J. 1979, An experimental study of effective teaching in first grade reading groups. *Elementary School Journal* 79, 193–223.

ANDERSSON, T. 1969, *Foreign Languages in the Elementary Schools: A Struggle Against Mediocrity*. Austin: University of Texas Press.

ANDRADE, C. and GING, D. 1988, Urban FLES models: Progress and promise. *Shaping the Future of Foreign Language Education: FLES, Articulation and Proficiency*. Lincolnwood, IL: National Textbook.

ASCHER, C. 1985, *Using Magnet Schools for Desegregation: Some Suggestions from the Research*. New York: Teachers College, Columbia University.

ATWELL, N. 1987, *In the Middle: Writing, Reading and Learning with Adolescents*. Portsmouth, NH: Boynton and Cook.

AUSUBEL, D.P., NOVAK, J.D. and HANESIAN, H. 1978, *Educational Psychology*. New York: Holt, Rinehart and Winston.

AVERY, C. 1987, First grade thinkers becoming literate. *Language Arts* 64, 611–18.

BARER-STEIN, T. 1987, Learning as a process of experiencing. *Studies in the Education of Adults* 19 (2), 87–108.

BARIK, H.C. and SWAIN, M. 1975, Three-year evaluation of a large scale early grade French immersion program: The Ottawa study. *Language Learning* 25 (1), 1–29.

BARRETT, T.C. 1972, Taxonomy of reading comprehension. *Reading 360 Monograph*. Lexington, MA: Ginn.

BAWDEN, R., BURKE, S. and DUFFY, G.G. 1979, *Teacher Conceptions of Reading and their Influence on Instruction*. East Lansing, MI: Institute for Research on Teaching, Michigan State University.

BENNETT, N. 1976, *Teaching Styles and Pupil Progress*. Cambridge, MA: Harvard University Press.

BERNHARDT, E.B. 1983, Testing foreign language reading comprehension: The immediate recall protocol. *Die Unterrichtspraxis* 16, 27–33.

BIBEAU, G. 1984, No easy road to bilingualism. In H. H. STERN (ed.) *Language and Society* 12 (4), 44–7.

BIDDLE, B.J. and ANDERSON, D.S. 1986, Theory, methods, knowledge and research on teaching. In M.C. WITTROCK (ed.) *Handbook of Research on Teaching* (pp. 230–52). New York: Macmillan.

BLOOM, B.S. 1956, *Taxonomy of Educational Objectives, Handbook I: Cognitive Domain.* New York: David McKay.

BOLTON, G. 1979, *Towards A Theory of Drama in Education.* Longman: London.

BRIDGE, C., WINOGRAD, P. and HALEY, D. 1983, Using predictable materials vs. preprimers to teach beginning sight words. *Reading Teacher* 36, 884–91.

BRUNER, J.S. 1960, *The Process of Education.* New York: Random House.

CAMPBELL, R.N., GRAY, T.C., RHODES, N.C. and SNOW, M.A. 1985, Foreign language learning in the elementary schools: A comparison of three language programs. *The Modern Language Journal* 69 (i), 44–54.

CAMBOURNE, B. 1984, Language, learning and literacy. In A. BUTLER and J. TURBILL (eds) *Toward a Reading-Writing Classroom* (pp. 5–10). Rozelle, NSW: Primary English Teaching Association.

CANALE, M. and SWAIN, M. 1980, Theoretical bases of communicative approaches to second language teaching and testing. *Applied Linguistics* 1 (4), 1–47.

CARR, W. and KEMMIS, S. 1983, *Becoming Critical: Knowing Through Action Research.* Victoria, Australia: Deakin University Press.

CHAUDRON, C. 1983, A descriptive model of discourse in the corrective treatment of learners' errors. In B.W. ROBINETT and J. SCHACHTER (eds.) *Second Language Learning: Contrastive Analysis, Error Analysis and Related Aspects (pp. 428–45). Ann Arbor: University of Michigan Press.*

CHOMSKY, N. 1972, *Language and Mind.* New York: Harcourt and Brace.

CLARK, C.M. 1978–79, A new question for research on teaching. *Educational Research Quarterly* 3 (4), 53–8.

— 1988, Asking the right questions about teacher preparation: Contributions of research on teacher thinking. *Educational Researcher* 17 (2), 5–12.

CLARK, C. and PETERSON, P. 1986, Teachers' thought processes. In M. C. WITROCK (ed.) *Handbook of Research in Education* (3rd edition) (pp. 255–96). New York: Macmillan.

CLARK, C.M. and ELMORE, J.L. 1979, *Teacher Planning in the First Weeks of School* (Research Series No. 56). East Lansing: Michigan State University, Institute for Research on Teaching. (ERIC Document Reproduction Service No. Ed 186 407).

CLARK, C.M. and LAMPERT, M. 1986, The study of teacher thinking: Implications for teacher education. *Journal of Teacher Education* 37 (5), 27–31.

CLARK, C. and YINGER, R. 1977, Research on teacher thinking. *Curriculum Inquiry* 7 (4), 279–304.

CLARK, C.M. and YINGER, R.J. 1987, Teacher planning. In D.C. BERLINER and B.V. ROSENSHINE (eds) *Talks to Teachers* (pp. 342–65). New York: Random House.

COHEN, A. 1974, The Culver City Spanish immersion program: The first two years. *Modern Language Journal* 58, 95–103.

COHEN, D. 1968, The effect of literature on vocabulary and reading achievement. *Elementary English* 45, 209–13, 217.

CONNELLY, F.M. and CLANDININ, D.J. 1990, Stories of experience and narrative inquiry. *Educational Researcher* 19 (5), 2–14.

COONEY, B. 1982, *Miss Rumphius.* New York: Viking.

CRAWFORD, J., GAGE, N.L., CORNO, L., STAYROOK, N., MITMAN, A., SCHUNK, D. and STALLINGS, J. 1978, *An Experiment on Teacher Effectiveness and Parent-Assisted Instruction in the Third Grade* Vols. 1–3. Stanford, CA: Center for Educational Research.

CUMMINS, J. and SWAIN, M. 1986, *Bilingualism in Education.* New York: Longman.

CURTAIN, H.A. and PESOLA, C.A. 1988, *Languages and Children-Making the Match: Foreign Language Instruction in the Elementary School.* Reading, MA: Addison-Wesley.

CZIKO, G.A. 1978, Differences in first-and second-language reading: The use of syntactic, semantic and discourse constraints. *Canadian Modern Language Review* 34 (3), 473–89.

— 1980, Language competence and reading strategies: A comparison of first- and second-language oral reading errors. *Language Learning* 30 (1), 101–16.

DI PIETRO, R. 1987, *Strategic Interaction: Learning Languages through Scenarios.* Cambridge: Cambridge University Press.

DOYLE, W. 1979, Making managerial decisions in classrooms. In D. L. DUKE (ed.) *Classroom Management* (78th yearbook of the National Society for the Study of Education, Part 2, pp. 42–74). Chicago: University of Chicago Press.

DUFFY, G.G. 1977, A study of teacher conceptions of reading. Paper presented at the Annual Meeting of the National Reading Conference. New Orleans. (ERIC Document Reproduction Service No. ED 151 763).

DULAY, H.C. and BURT, M.K. 1972, Goofing: An indicator of children's second language learning strategies. *Language Learning* 22 (2), 235–52.

DUNKIN, M.J. and BIDDLE, B.J. 1974, *The Study of Teaching.* New York: Holt, Rinehart and Winston.

ELBAZ, F. 1981, Practical knowledge: Report of a case study. *Curriculum Inquiry* 11 (1), 43–71.

ELLEY, W. 1989, Vocabulary acquisition from listening to stories. *Reading Research Quarterly* 24, 174–87.

ERVIN-TRIPP, S.M. 1974, Is second language learning like the first? *TESOL Quarterly* 8 (2), 111–27.

GAARDER, B. 1978, The golden rules of second language acquisition by young children. *NABE Journal* 59–60.

GAGE, N. and GIACONIA, R. 1981, Teaching practices and student achievement: Causal connections. *New York University Education Quarterly* 13 (iii), 2–9.

GENESEE, F. 1983, Bilingual education of majority language children: The immersion experiments in review. *Applied Psycholinguistics* 4, 1–46.

— 1987, *Learning through Two Languages.* Cambridge, MA: Newbury House Publishers.

GENESEE, F., HOLOBOW, N., LAMBERT, W.E., CLEGHORN, A. and WALLING, R. 1985, The linguistic and academic development of English-speaking children in French schools: Grade 4 outcomes. *Canadian Modern Language Review* 41 (4), 669–85.

GINSBURG, M. 1972, *The Chick and the Duckling.* New York: Macmillan.

GOOD, T.L. and GROUWS, D.A. 1979, The Missouri mathematics effectiveness project: An experimental study in fourth grade classrooms. *Journal of Educational Psychology* 71, 335–62.

GOODMAN, K. 1986, *What's Whole in Whole Language?* Portsmouth, NH: Heinemann.

GRAY, V.A. 1986, A summary of the elementary school evaluation of the early French immersion program. *Canadian Modern Language Review* 42 (5), 940–51.

GREEN, J. and HARKER, J. 1988, *Multiple Perspective Analysis of Classroom Discourse.* Norwood, NJ: Ablex Publishing Co.

GUNTERMANN, G. and PHILLIPS, J.K. 1982, *Functional-Notional Concepts: Adapting the FL Textbook.* Washington: Center for Applied Linguistics.

HAKUTA, K. 1974, Prefabricated patterns and the emergence of structure in second language acquisition. *Language Learning* 24, 287–98.

HALLIDAY, M.A.K. 1973, *Explorations in the Functions of Language.* London: Edward Arnold.

HALLIDAY, M. 1975, *Learning How to Mean: Explorations in the Functions of Language.* London: Edward Arnold.

HAMMADOU, J. and BERNHARDT, E. 1987, On being and becoming a foreign language teacher. *Theory into Practice* 26 (3), 301–6.

HAMMERLY, H. 1987, The immersion approach: Litmus test of second language acquisition through classroom communication. *The Modern Language Journal* 71 (4), 395–401.

HARLEY, B. 1984, How good is their French? In H. H. STERN (ed.) *Language and Society* 12, 55–60.

HARLEY, B., ALLEN, P., CUMMINS, J. and SWAIN, M. 1990, *The Development of Second Language Proficiency.* Cambridge: Cambridge.

HECHINGER, F.M. 1981, *Education Agenda for the 1980s.* Bloomington, IN: Phi Delta Kappa Educational Foundation.

HICKMAN. J. 1981, A new perspective on response to literature: Research in an elementary school setting. *Research in the Teaching of English* 15, 343–54.

— 1983, Classrooms that help children like books. In N. ROSER and M. FRITH (eds) *Children's Choices: Teaching with Books Children Like* (pp. 1–11). Newark, DE: International Reading Association.

HOLMES GROUP. 1986, *Tomorrow's Teachers: A Report on the Holmes Group.* East Lansing, MI: Holmes Group.

JANESICK, V. 1979, *An Ethnographic Study of a Teacher's Classroom Perspective: Implications for Curriculum.* (Research Series No. 33). East Lansing, MI: Institute for Research on Teaching, Michigan State University.

JOHNSON, L. and O'NEILL, C. 1984, *Dorothy Heathcote: Collected Writings on Educational Drama.* Hutchinson: London.

KRASHEN, S.D. 1981, *Second Language Acquisition and Second Language Learning.* Oxford: Pergamon Press.

— 1982, *Principles and Practice in Second Language Acquisition.* Oxford: Pergamon Press.

— 1984, Immersion: Why it works and what it has taught us. The French immersion phenomenon. In H. H. STERN (ed.) *Language and Society* (Special Issue) 12, 61–4.

— 1985a, *The Input Hypothesis*. London: Longman.

— 1985b, Inquiries and Insights. Hayward, CA: Alemany.

LAMBERT, W.E. and TUCKER, G.R. 1972, *The Bilingual Education of Children*. Rowley, MA: Newbury House Publishers.

LAPKIN, S. 1984, How well do immersion students speak and write French? *Canadian Modern Language Review* 40 (5), 575–85.

LAPKIN, S. and SWAIN, M. with SHAPSON, S. 1990, French immersion research agenda for the 90s. *Canadian Modern Language Review* 46 (4), 638–74.

LEHR, S. 1988, The child's developing sense of theme as a response to literature. *Reading Research Quarterly* 23, 337–56.

LENNEBERG, E. 1967, *Biological Foundations of Language*. New York: John Wiley.

LINCOLN, Y.S. and GUBA, E.G. 1985, *Naturalistic Inquiry*. Beverly Hills, CA: Sage Publications.

LIPTON, G.C. 1988, *Practical Handbook to Elementary Foreign Language Programs: Including FLES, FLEX and Immersion Programs*. Lincolnwood, IL: National Textbook Company.

LONG, M. 1981, Input, interaction and second language acquisition. In H. WINITS (ed.) *Native Language and Foreign Language Acquisition* (Annals of the New York Academy of Sciences) 379, 259–78.

LONG, M.H. and SATO, C.J. 1983, Classroom foreigner talk discourse: Forms and functions of teachers' questions. In H.W. SELIGER and M.H. LONG (eds.) *Classroom Oriented Research in Second Language Acquisition* (pp. 268–85). Rowley, MA: Newbury House.

LYSTER, R. 1987, Speaking immersion. *The Canadian Modern Language Review* 43 (4), 701–17.

— 1990, The role of analytic language teaching in French immersion programs. *The Canadian Modern Language Review* 47 (1), 159–75.

MACKEY, W.F. 1978, The importation of bilingual education models. In J. ALATIS (ed.) *Georgetown University Roundtable—International Dimensions of Bilingual Education* (pp. 1–18). Washington, DC: Georgetown University Press.

MACLACHLAN, P. 1985, *Sarah, Plain and Tall*. New York: Harper.

MAJHANOVICH, S. and FISH, S. 1988, Training French immersion teachers for the primary grades: An experimental course at the University of Western Ontario. *Foreign Language Annals* 4, 311–19.

MARTIN, B., Jr 1983, *Brown Bear, Brown Bear, What Do You See?* New York: Holt.

MATHISON, S. 1988, Why triangulate? *Educational Researcher* 17 (2), 13–17.

MCCLURE, A., HARRISON, P. and REED, S. 1990, *Sunrises and Songs: Reading and Writing Poetry in an Elementary Classroom*. Portsmouth, NJ: Heinemann.

MCMILLAN, C.B. 1980, *Magnet Schools: An Approach to Voluntary Desegregation*. Bloomington, IN: Phi Delta Kappa Educational Foundation.

MCNEILL, D. 1970, *The Acquisition of Language: The Study of Developmental Psycholinguistics*. New York: Harper and Row.

MCRAE, J. 1985, *Using Drama in the Classroom*. New York: Pergamon.

MET, M. 1987, Twenty questions: The most commonly asked questions about starting an immersion program. *Foreign Language Annals* 20, 311–15.

MET, M. and RHODES, N. 1990, Elementary foreign language instruction: Priorities for the 1990s. *Foreign Language Annals* 23, 433–43.

MILLS, H. and CLYDE, J. 1990, *Portraits of Whole Language Classrooms: Learning for All Ages*. Portsmouth, NJ: Heinemann.

MOHAN, B.A. 1986, *Language and Content*. Reading, MA: Addison-Wesley.

MORINE-DERSHIMER, G. 1978–79a, How teachers "see" their pupils. *Educational Research Quarterly* 3 (4), 43–52.

— 1978–79b, The anatomy of teacher prediction. *Educational Research Quarterly* 3 (4), 59–65.

MORRISON, F. and PAWLEY, C. 1986, *Evaluation of the Second Language Learning (French) Programs in the Schools of the Ottawa and Carleton Boards of Education, Volume 1: French Proficiency of Immersion Students at the Grade 12 Level*. Toronto: Ministry of Education.

MORROW, L. and WEINSTEIN, C. 1986, Encouraging voluntary reading: The impact of a literature program on children's use of library centers. *Reading Research Quarterly* 21, 330–46.

NATIONAL COMMISSION ON EXCELLENCE IN EDUCATION 1983, *A Nation at Risk: The Imperative for Educational Reform*. Washington, DC: US Government Printing Office. Report No. 0655-000-00177.

NEELANDS, J. 1984, *Making Sense of Drama*. Portsmouth, NH: Heinemann.

NESPOR, J. 1984, *Issues in the Study of Teachers' Goals and Intentions in the Classroom* (R & D Report No. 8022). Texas University, Austin. Research and Development Center for Teacher Education. (ERIC Document Reproduction Service No. ED 260 075).

NEWKIRK, T. 1989, *More than Stories: The Range of Children's Writing*. Portsmouth, NJ: Heinemann.

NUNAN, D. 1987, *The Learner Centered Curriculum*. Cambridge: Cambridge University Press.

— 1989, *Designing Tasks for the Communicative Classroom*. Cambridge Language Teaching Library.

O'NEILL, C. and LAMBERT, A. 1982, *Drama Structures*. London: Hutchinson.

PAWLEY, C. 1985, How bilingual are French immersion students. *The Canadian Modern Language Review* 41 (5), 865–76.

PELLERIN, M. and HAMMERLY, H. 1986, L'expression orale après treize ans d'immersion française [Oral expression after thirteen years of French immersion]. *Canadian Modern Language Review* 42 (3), 592–606.

PENFIELD, W. and ROBERTS, L. 1959, *Speech and Brain Mechanisms*. New York: Atheneum.

PETERSON, P.L. and CLARK, C.M. 1978, Teachers' reports of their cognitive processes during teaching. *American Educational Research Journal* 15, 555–65.

PICA, T. and DOUGHTY, C. 1985, Input and interaction in the communicative language classroom: A comparison of teacher-fronted and group activities. In S.M. GASS and C.G. MADDEN (eds) *Input in Second Language Acquisition* (pp. 115–32). Rowley, MA: Newbury House.

PORTER, P.A. 1986, How learners talk to each other: Input and interaction in task-centered discussions. In R.R. DAY (ed.) *Talking to Learn: Conversation in Second Language Acquisition* (pp. 200–22). Rowley, MA: Newbury House.

PRABHU, N. 1987, *Second Language Pedagogy*. Oxford University Press.

PRESIDENT'S COMMISSION ON FOREIGN LANGUAGE AND INTERNATIONAL STUDIES 1979, Strength through wisdom: A critique of U.S. capability. *Modern Language Journal* 64 (4), 9–57.

REUTZEL, D. and FAWSON, P. 1989, Using a literature webbing strategy lesson with predictable books. Reading Teacher 43, 208–15.

RICHARDS, J.C. 1990, The dilemma of teacher education in second language teaching. In J. C. RICHARDS and D. NUNAN (eds) *Second Language Teacher Education* (pp. 3–15). New York: Cambridge.

RICHARDS, J.C. and NUNAN, D. (eds) 1990, *Second Language Teacher Education*. New York: Cambridge.

RIDLEY, L. 1990, Whole language in the ESL classroom. In H. MILLS and J. CLYDE (eds) *Portraits of Whole Language Classrooms: Learning for All Ages* (pp. 213–28). Portsmouth, NJ: Heinemann.

RIORDAN, R.C. 1972, *Alternative Schools in Action*. Bloomington, IN: Phi Delta Kappa Educational Foundation.

ROSER, N., HOFFMAN, J. and FAREST, C. 1990, Language, literature and at-risk children. *Reading Teacher* 43, 112–20.

RULON, K.A. and MCCREARY, J. 1986, Negotiation on content: Teacher-fronted and small-group interaction. In R.R. DAY (ed.) *Talking to Learn: Conversation in Second Language Acquisition* (pp. 182–99). Rowley, MA: Newbury House.

SALOMONE, A. M. 1989, A descriptive analysis of teacher thinking in an elementary French Immersion School. Unpublished doctoral dissertation. The Ohio State University, Columbus, Ohio.

SAVILLE-TROIKE, M. 1985, Cultural input in second language learning. In S.M. GASS and C.G. MADDEN (eds) *Input in Second Language Acquisition* (pp. 51–8). Rowley, MA: Newbury House.

SCHRIER, L.L. 1990, On becoming an elementary foreign language teacher. *FLES News* 6 (i), 1–5.

SELIGER, H.W. 1983, Learner interaction in the classroom and its effect on language acquisition. In H.W. SELIGER and M.H. LONG (eds) *Classroom Oriented Research in Second Language Acquisition* (pp. 246–65). Rowley, MA: Newbury House.

SELINKER, L., SWAIN, M. and DUMAS, G. 1975, The interlanguage hypothesis extended to children. *Language Learning* 25 (1), 139–52.

SHAVELSON, R. and STERN, P. 1981, Research on teachers' pedagogical thoughts, judgments, decisions and behavior. *Review of Educational Research* 51, 455–98.

SMITH, V., BURKE, D.J. and BARR, R.D. 1974, *Optional Alternative Public Schools*. Bloomington, IN: Phi Delta Kappa Educational Foundation.

SMITH, S. 1984, *The Theatre Arts and the Teaching of Second Languages*. Reading, MA: Addison-Wesley.

SNOW, M.A. 1987, *Immersion Teacher Handbook*. Los Angeles: Center for Language Education and Research.

SPILKA, I. 1976, Assessment of second-language performance in immersion programs. *Canadian Modern Language Review* 32 (5), 543–61.

STALLINGS, J., NEEDELS, M. and STAYROOK, N. 1979, *How to Change the Process of Teaching Basic Reading Skills in Secondary Schools. Final Report to the National Institute of Education.* Menlo Park, CA: SRI International.

STEPHENS, D., HUNTSMAN, R., O'NEILL, K., STORY, J., WATSON, V. and TOOMES, J. 1990, We call it good teaching. In H. MILLS and J. CLYDE (eds) *Portraits of Whole Language Classrooms: Learning for All Ages* (pp. 275–99). Portsmouth, NH: Heinemann.

STERN, H.H. 1978, French immersion in Canada: Achievements and directions. *Canadian Modern Language Review* 34 (5), 836–54.

SWAIN, M. 1978, French immersion: Early, late or partial? *Canadian Modern Language Review* 34, 577–85.

— 1982, Immersion education: Applicability for nonvernacular teaching to vernacular speakers. In B. HARTFORD, A. VALDMAN and C.R. FOSTER (eds) *Issues in International Bilingual Education: The Role of the Vernacular* (pp. 81–97). New York: Plenum Press.

— 1985, Communicative competence: Some roles of comprehensible input and comprehensible output in its development. In S.M. GASS and C.G. MADDEN (eds) *Input in Second Language Acquisition* (pp. 235–53). Rowley, MA: Newbury House.

SWAIN, M. and BARIK, H.C. 1976, *Five Years of Primary French Immersion.* Toronto: University of Toronto Press.

SWAIN, M. and LAPKIN, S. 1982, *Evaluating Bilingual Education: A Canadian Case Study.* Toronto: Ontario Institute for Studies in Education.

VAN DONGEN, R. 1987, Children's narrative thought, at home and at school. *Language Arts* 64, 79–87.

WAGNER, B. 1976, *Dorothy Heathcote: Drama as a Learning Medium.* National Education Association Publication. Washington, DC.

WATKINS, B.T. 1989, Foreign-language instruction is being revitalized as faculty members stress 'doing' over 'knowing'. *The Chronicle of Higher Education* February 22, 1989.

WENDEN, A. and RUBIN, J. 1987, *Learner Strategies in Language Learning.* Englewood Cliffs, NJ: Prentice-Hall.

WESTPHAL, P. 1989, What I learned in second grade: A French teacher's experience. *FLES News* 3 (i), 1–8.

WIDDOWSON, H. 1978, *Teaching Language as Communication.* Oxford: OUP.

WILLETTS, K.F. (ed.) 1986, *Integrating Language and Content Instruction.* Proceedings of the Seminar. Los Angeles: Center for Language Education and Research. (January 6, 1986). (ERIC Document Reproduction No. ED 278 262).

WOLLMAN-BONILLA, J. 1989, Reading journals: Invitations to participate in literature. *Reading Teacher* 43, 112–20.

WONG-FILLMORE, L. 1985, When does teacher talk work as input? In S.M. GASS and C.G. MADDEN (eds) *Input in Second Language Acquisition* (pp. 17–50). Rowley, MA: Newbury House.

YINGER, R.J. 1979, Routines in teacher planning. *Theory into Practice* 18 (3), 163–9.

Index